TRACING GOD'S
STORY WORKBOOK

TRACING GOD'S STORY WORKBOOK

An Introduction to
Biblical Theology

JON NIELSON

WHEATON, ILLINOIS

Tracing God's Story Workbook: An Introduction to Biblical Theology

© 2024 by Jon Nielson

Published by Crossway
         1300 Crescent Street
         Wheaton, Illinois 60187

Cover design: Zach DeYoung

First printing 2024

Printed in Colombia

Trade paperback ISBN: 978-1-4335-8742-9

Crossway is a publishing ministry of Good News Publishers.

NP			32	31	30	29	28	27	26	25	24
14	13	12	11	10	9	8	7	6	5	4	3	2	1

CONTENTS

INTRODUCTION

This workbook is intended to be used as a companion to the book *Tracing God's Story: An Introduction to Biblical Theology.* I hope that it will be useful to you as you get to know the Bible as *one unified story of God's redemptive work through his Son, Jesus Christ.*

That, really, is the purpose of this project: I hope to help God's people see the wonderful unity of Scripture that was intended by the divine author who inspired each of the human biblical authors. The Bible is made up of sixty-six books, written by more than forty human authors, and yet it tells a remarkably unified story of God's creation, humanity's fall, God's great saving work through his Son Jesus, and the ultimate hope for restoration—a final judgment, and then a new heaven and new earth where God's people will live with him forever. I hope the book—and this workbook—will help you study the Bible as one grand story!

To get the most out of this workbook, I encourage you to work through it as you read the book (and the biblical passages) carefully and thoroughly. Answer the questions fully and thoughtfully; the harder you work, the more you'll get out of this study. We'll begin in the book of Genesis and trace the story of the Bible all the way through to Revelation, seeking to keep in mind our place in the story at each step along the way.

It is my hope and prayer that by the end of your work through *Tracing God's Story,* you will understand the shape of Scripture more fully and love God's word more than ever before.

WHAT IS BIBLICAL THEOLOGY?

What exactly is *biblical theology*? Biblical theology is a discipline that seeks to discover theology (truth about God and his work) through the gradual and progressive revelation of his saving plan in the story of the Bible. This is often done by tracing certain themes or ideas through Scripture from beginning to end—Genesis to Revelation.

The core conviction of those who practice the discipline of biblical theology is that the Bible is one unified work—a book inspired by one divine author (God) and given to human beings to help them understand his broad saving plan, which ultimately was accomplished through the death and resurrection of his Son, Jesus Christ. We will see how Jesus himself pointed toward this kind of understanding of Scripture.

So our goal in this workbook (and the accompanying book) is to do biblical theology. We will trace God's story of redemption as it is revealed progressively in Scripture.

Respond to the following questions as you begin your study of biblical theology:

1. How did Peter, in his sermon at Pentecost (see Acts 2), use the Old Testament to point to a right understanding of Jesus Christ?

---

2. How does Peter's approach affect the way that we should expect to read and understand a book like Psalms in the Old Testament?

3. What was the response of the people in Jerusalem when they heard Peter's sermon?

FOUNDATIONS FOR BIBLICAL THEOLOGY

Review pages 2–3 in *Tracing God's Story*

Why do we affirm that the Bible is one story of God's saving work in the world? Why do we insist that Jesus Christ is the key to understanding the Bible—the very center of the Bible story? Why does biblical theology seek to understand God's unfolding plan of salvation, which is progressively revealed in Scripture? One answer to these questions, which you'll see in your Bible reading, is this: *Jesus himself* read and interpreted the Old Testament in this way. When we practice biblical theology, we are following the lead of Jesus in the way that he looked at and applied the Old Testament Scriptures.

1. What did Jesus say about his suffering and death to the two men who met him on the road to Emmaus after his resurrection (Luke 24:25–27)?

2. What does Luke say that Jesus did next? How does Luke describe the "sermon" that Jesus gave to the two men (Luke 24:28–32)?

_____

_____

_____

_____

3. What does this passage mean for us as we consider the discipline of biblical theology?

_____

_____

_____

_____

The Apostles' Preaching

Review pages 5–6 in *Tracing God's Story*

In his sermon in Acts 2, Peter used Old Testament Scriptures—specifically, the Psalms and the prophet Joel—to show what was really happening on the day of Pentecost: God's promised Spirit was being poured out as he had promised through Joel and in accordance with David's descendant being raised from the dead and crowned king (Ps. 16). Acts 2, then, is another key passage for helping us understand that biblical theology, according to Jesus *and* his apostles, is a good, right, and legitimate way to study the Bible. In fact, according to Peter, it is really the *only* way to understand the Bible correctly. We do not "get" Joel unless we see how his words were fulfilled in the day of Pentecost. We do not "get" David, in Psalm 16, if we do not see the beautiful way that his words were fulfilled in the death and resurrection of Jesus Christ.

1. In what ways did Peter connect the work of Jesus Christ to the promises of God in the Old Testament? What passages did he quote as he explained what Jesus accomplished?

_____

_____

---

2. How did Peter use Psalm 16? In what ways did Peter claim that this psalm pointed ahead to the resurrection of Jesus Christ?

---

3. What does Peter's approach to this sermon tell us about the way we should read the Old Testament?

Old Testament "Pointers"

Review pages 6–7 in *Tracing God's Story*

God intentionally designed Old Testament rituals to point us to Christ. This is clearly the argument of the author of the book of Hebrews. The way that God set things up under the Levitical priesthood was not random. It was meant to show God's people about the need for Christ's work and to teach them about the final salvation that was coming in God's own Son. This means we can learn much about Christ and his work by understanding the Old Testament. A careful study of the priestly duties and functions, for example, can teach us about what Jesus accomplished for sinners on the cross.

Therefore, biblical theology reminds us that all of Scripture is valuable for showing us the beauty of the gospel. All of the Bible is from God, and it is all meant to show Christ in all his beauty, glory, and salvation to lost sinners.

1. In what way does the author of Hebrews describe the priestly ministry of Jesus Christ (see Heb. 8)?

---

2. How does this passage use the Old Testament role and picture of a priest to show us the beauty and power of Jesus's work?

---

3. What can this passage teach us about our approach to the Old Testament?

The Unity of the Bible

Review pages 7–8 in *Tracing God's Story*

As we look at the book of Revelation, we begin to see an important foundation for biblical theology: the Bible story ends in a way that relates to all that has come before. There are echoes of Genesis in Revelation, as well as pictures and events from every part of the story of God's saving work in the lives of his people in the world. When we read Revelation in this way and see how closely it is connected to all that has come before in the Bible story (Old Testament and New Testament), it is very difficult to not see that the Bible really does come to us as one unified story of God's great saving work in the world—a work that is centered on his Son, Jesus Christ. The Bible is God's great story, and it hangs together perfectly.

1. What aspects of the descriptions of the perfect city in Revelation 21–22—this new heaven and new earth—connect to other parts of the Bible story with which you are familiar?

2. What do these connections tell you about the Bible as one unified work—one big story of God's saving work in the world?

3. How is this passage evidence for the legitimacy of the discipline of biblical theology?

THE VALUE OF BIBLICAL THEOLOGY

Review pages 9–10 in *Tracing God's Story*

Biblical theology is most helpful for understanding the big picture of the storyline of the Bible. Since biblical theological study moves through the Bible from Genesis to Revelation, it offers the best opportunity to get to know Scripture as it develops. Biblical theology studies the Bible as it is revealed to us—not in systematic categories, but in books—in one developing story. It can help students see the centrality of the gospel in not just the New Testament but all of Scripture. Biblical theology helps us remember that the Bible tells the unified story of the work of one God in one world throughout all of history.

1. What do we learn from Jesus's words in Luke 4:16–30 about his understanding of his role and ministry in relation to Old Testament prophecy?

_____

_____

_____

_____

2. Why is this passage a good example of Jesus himself "doing" biblical theology?

_____

_____

_____

_____

3. How would you argue that biblical theology is an important discipline for Christians—alongside systematic and historical theology?

_____

_____

_____

_____

THE "JOURNEY" OF BIBLICAL THEOLOGY

Review pages 10–11 in *Tracing God's Story*

If we fail to make the full "journey" in our study of biblical theology, we will almost certainly fall into one or more mistakes when trying to understand what the Bible means.

If we miss "text to context," we will ignore important historical details and end up with a generic, misleading impression of a text. If we miss "context to Christ," we will ignore how each story points us toward the central theme in all Scripture. And if we miss "Christ to us," we will fail to properly apply the meaning of Scripture to our lives as Christians. We need to take every step as we study every passage in the Bible.

1. Why might some people be tempted to skip an important step in studying the Bible—and which steps tend to be skipped most often, in your opinion?

2. How is it helpful for students of the Bible to take the full journey of biblical theological study, moving all the way from the text of Scripture itself to the historical context to the legitimate connection to Jesus Christ and finally to the implications for our lives as we follow him?

BIBLICAL THEOLOGY AND THE GOSPEL

Review pages 12–13 in *Tracing God's Story*

A careful study of the progressive revealing of God's saving work in the world begins to show us how central the gospel must be to a right understanding of all of Scripture. We begin to see, through a biblical theological perspective, that the Old Testament cannot be rightly understood without its proper fulfillment in—and connection to—the gospel. When we see the Bible as one connected story, written by God and focusing on the climax of his work in Jesus Christ, we begin to understand how every part of this story ultimately makes sense only as it relates to Jesus. There is simply no other way of bringing together the sixty-six books of the Bible; they make sense as they center around the life, death, and resurrection of Jesus.

1. Paul repeats the phrase "in accordance with the Scriptures" twice in his explanation of the gospel in 1 Corinthians 15:1–4. What is the significance of this phrase? What is Paul saying about the work of Jesus Christ as it relates to the rest of the Bible?

2. How can Jesus's death on the cross be "in accordance with the Scriptures"? What does this mean?

BIBLICAL THEOLOGY AND PERSONAL BIBLE STUDY

Review pages 14–15 in *Tracing God's Story*

It is the study of biblical theology that can best help you—as a follower of God today—place yourself in the story of God's work in the world that has been going on since his creation of Adam and Eve. Through studying the Bible as one great story, with one author and one great Savior, we begin to see that we are living in the final chapter of that story—along with God's people who followed Jesus from the first days of the early church till now. Through faith in Jesus Christ, we become part of the people God has formed through all times and in all places. We begin to realize that we really can know and worship the God of Abraham and Moses; we will share eternal life with David, Jacob, and Daniel!

1. If you assumed that the doctrine of inspiration was *not* true, and that Psalm 16 was a random poem with no connection to the rest of the Bible, how might you interpret it? What would you make of verse 10? Would you be able to explain it?

2. What changes about the interpretation of this psalm when you see the Bible as one story, with its climax in Jesus Christ as the eternal King and Savior?

RECAP

We see from the example of Jesus Christ himself that it is legitimate to read the Bible as one story woven together in all of its parts by the sovereign and saving purposes of God. We trust God—the divine author of Scripture—that his word is unified and consistent throughout all its parts.

SO WHAT?

As you conclude this chapter, jot down answers to the following application questions:

1. In what ways are the foundations of biblical theology (from Jesus and the apostles) personally encouraging to you?

2. How can these foundations help you grow in your faith?

_____

_____

_____

_____

THE OLD TESTAMENT

GOD'S CREATION AND A CRISIS
PART 1

In chapter 2 of *Tracing God's Story*, we begin to move through the big story of the Bible. The story begins with God's creation of all things, which is followed quickly by a terrible crisis (as we will see in chapter 3).

THE GOD WHO CREATES

Review pages 20–21 in *Tracing God's Story*

The account of creation, ultimately, is the foundation and starting point for the big story of God's work in the world. It sets God up as the Creator, and everything else in the story flows out of this foundational truth. The most basic acknowledgment that humans can make as they seek to relate to God—as well as discover their purpose, meaning in life, and calling— is that God is the Creator and they are his creatures. There is a huge distinction between everything that has been created—including human beings—and the infinitely wise and powerful Creator of the universe. Before a man or woman even begins to get to know God, it is important to start with this basic admission: "I am a creature, made by the Creator God."

1. What are some of your observations about the first two verses in the Bible? What jumps out at you immediately from these verses?

....

....

2. What is the significance of the fact that the Bible begins with God as the Creator of the heavens and the earth? What are some of the implications of this simple, but huge, truth?

....

....

....

....

THE ETERNAL CREATOR GOD

Review pages 21–22 in *Tracing God's Story*

Genesis 1 begins simply with these words: "In the beginning, God . . ." This simple introduction to this book—and to the entire Bible—reminds us of an incredibly significant fact: the God who created this world and us has existed forever in eternal glory, splendor, and power. There has never been a time—ever—when God did not exist. There was a time when you did not yet exist. There was a time when this entire world—even the whole universe—did not exist. God, though, is eternal; he has always existed in his perfect being, glory, and holiness. This concept stretches our minds, but it remains far beyond our capacity as humans to completely grasp it. In the beginning, before anything existed, God was there; he chose to create the universe and the reality that we now know and see all around us.

1. According to Genesis 1:1, what sets God apart from everything else in the universe? Why is this truth so significant for us to understand?

....

....

....

....

2. What is the right response to the God who has existed from eternity and who created the heavens and the earth, according to Revelation 4?

_____

_____

_____

_____

3. What are some ways that you can apply these passages to your life today—particularly in the way that you think about (and approach) the one true God?

_____

_____

_____

_____

GOD CREATES *EX NIHILO* BY SPEAKING

Review pages 23–25 in *Tracing God's Story*

Genesis 1 and Hebrews 11 teach the important and fundamental truth that when God created the world, he created it out of *nothing*. This doctrine is often referred to as creation *ex nihilo*, or "out of nothing." It means that when God created the universe, he did not use any materials that were "lying around" in order to form things. He literally made physical things—tangible reality—appear out of thin air—although there was not even air before the world existed! Furthermore, God did not create the world with his "hands." Hebrews, as well as the rest of the Genesis creation account, tells us this important truth: God created the universe by the power of his word. God *spoke* the world into existence. This simple but profound truth has incredible implications for the rest of the story of the Bible, especially as it relates to the power and effectiveness of God's word. We serve a God who literally spoke reality into existence. His word is incredibly powerful; it has *creative* power. This is truly a great God; he is the rightful King of all.

Notice, too, the amazing order that God displayed as he created the world. Carefully, with great wisdom, he ordained each "light" in the "expanse" of the heavens (Gen. 1:14–15) to have its proper place and time, and he separated the land from the waters in perfect ratios. God, we see, is a God of careful planning and wise ordering of every detail of his creation. As the account of God's creation goes on, we see that he is completely in control of every aspect. He speaks and things happen. Lights appear in the heavens; waters swarm with living creatures; animals begin to fill the earth. God is the one with all authority and power in every inch of creation. He is sovereign, powerful, and completely in control.

1. How did God create the world, according to Hebrews 11? Why is this so hard for us to understand and imagine?

2. What do we learn about God from Genesis 1, which records his creation of the world?

3. How do you see the order and organization of a wise God, as it is revealed in Genesis 1?

THE GOODNESS OF CREATION

Review pages 27–28 in *Tracing God's Story*

The world in which we live was not thrown together haphazardly by a God who was trying to make something in a hurry! The fact that God stopped, admired his creation, and called it "good" several times in Genesis 1 tells us that he made it with great care, attention to detail, and beauty. God was very intentional about his creation; he worked to make it good in exactly the way he intended. Think about this for a moment: the God of the universe stopped, admired his work, and declared it to be good. That is amazing.

In addition, we can see from these repeated phrases that God was very pleased with this world that he had made. He had not created it from any need that he had for companionship or entertainment; yet he delighted in it. The creation brought delight to the heart of the Creator who had made it all to be "good."

1. What are some of the repeated phrases that you observe in the creation account? List them here.

---

2. What is the significance of the repeated phrase "And God saw that it was good"? Why is that an important phrase in this account?

---

3. What can we conclude about God's world based on this repeated phrase?

GOD CREATES HUMANS IN THE *IMAGO DEI*

Review pages 28–30 in *Tracing God's Story*

Human beings are special. I don't mean they are special in a "feel-good" way—the way that parents tell their toddlers that they are special. I mean that humans are special and dear to God in a way that is set apart from every other part of his creation. God actively and personally engaged in the creation of human beings in a special way. That means they are unique. They are distinct from the animal world—set apart by the Creator God as uniquely intelligent and designed beings. Indeed, human beings are the focal point of God's creation.

Genesis 1:27 tells us that human beings were created in "the image of God" (the *imago Dei*). This does not mean that we literally resemble God physically. But it does mean that we reflect him in some ways; we are "like" God—not perfectly, but in ways that reflect the way that he really is. The text of Genesis also tells us that human beings were made as "male and female," and both genders are in the image of God. Our personalities, capacities, and relationships point to him in significant ways.

1. What aspects of the way that God talked about the creation of human beings sets apart this phase of creation as more personal to him than all the rest?

2. How did God, in Genesis 1, describe the creation of human beings? What is the language that he uses as he talks to "himself" in the context of the Trinity?

3. In Psalm 8, how does David express the exalted place that God gave to human beings in his creation? How does Psalm 8 help us understand the glorious role of human beings in this world that God has made?

HUMANS' ROLE IN CREATION

Review pages 32–33 in *Tracing God's Story*

God gave Adam and Eve instructions to "multiply" and fill the earth (Gen. 1:28). God's goal in the creation of men and women was obviously to have them create a great race of human beings—people for his own glory and pleasure. This creation "mandate" tells human beings to create more human beings in order to fill the earth with people made in God's image. God also called human beings to "subdue" the earth and to have "dominion" over all the other living creatures on the earth (v. 28).

1. What is surprising to you about God's "charge" to human beings in Genesis 1:28–31? Does anything stand out to you in a new way as you read this passage?

2. In Psalm 8, how does David explain God's intended role for human beings? What is David's response to God as he considers this great responsibility?

GOD'S REST

Review pages 34–35 in *Tracing God's Story*

Genesis 2:2 tells us that God rested on the seventh day of the creation week. This means that God intentionally *stopped* his work of creation. In other words, his creative work in this world was finished. God is still working in many ways, but after the sixth day ended, he really did stop his work of creation in the world and declared it to be "very good" (1:31). Since God rested on the seventh day of his creation, he commanded his people to take a day of rest from their work each week too—a "holy" day that would be devoted not only to rest but also to the worship of their God (2:3).

1. What seems to have been the reason for God's rest on the seventh day? Does the text of Genesis 1–2 give us any explanation for this?

2. How did God give special significance to this seventh day? How does Genesis 2 show us this?

3. What do you know about the relationship of the "Sabbath" to this seventh day of creation?

....

....

⬡ RECAP

In this chapter, we've started with the fundamental truths of the Bible story: God is the almighty Creator of all things, including human beings, whom he made in his image and for his glory. As Creator and King, God defines what is right and good for all his creation. The story of the Bible begins there—and so must we, as we seek to get a sense of the big picture of Scripture.

⬇ SO WHAT?

As you conclude this chapter, jot down answers to the following application question:

1. God is the Creator and King of this world. What implications of this truth for the world, human beings, and yourself can you think of? Write down as many as you can.

....

....

....

....

GOD'S CREATION AND A CRISIS
PART 2

After relating the story of God's creation of the world, Genesis shows us a beautiful picture of what life was like in the garden of Eden, the center of God's good creation. Sadly, that picture soon became distorted when sin entered the world—the first crisis in the story of the Bible.

A GOOD WORLD AND GOOD WORK

Review pages 39–41 in *Tracing God's Story*

Genesis shows us the perfect place that God provided for his people to live. Consider some of the descriptions of the garden of Eden that we see in Genesis: God caused a mist to come up from the ground, which watered the whole earth, providing nourishment and hydration to the trees, plants, and vegetation (Gen. 2:6). God gave good food for people to eat, causing trees and plants to spring up in the garden (v. 9). In addition, there were two special trees in the garden—the tree of life and the tree of the knowledge of good and evil. God intentionally and personally formed human beings in his image and set them to rule over this beautiful and perfect place.

Genesis 2:15 tells us that God set Adam to work in the garden of Eden and commanded him to "keep" it carefully. This means that, when we picture Adam in the garden of Eden, we should see him hard at work taking care of the plants and animals, gathering food along with Eve, and enjoying this good work that God had given to him. Work came from God *before* man's fall into sin. That means work is a good thing; it is a gift from the Creator. Work brings purpose; ultimately, all human beings want to have work that is fulfilling and enjoyable.

1. As you read the restatement of the creation of Adam in Genesis 2:4–14, what new insights do you get about God's creation of him? How does this passage show us, even more clearly, God's personal and intentional engagement with human beings in his creation?

2. As you look at this passage, what do you learn about what God called Adam to do in the garden of Eden?

3. How might this short passage show us the pattern for the way God rules his people and calls them to live in his world?

THE CREATION OF EVE

Review pages 41–43 in *Tracing God's Story*

God created Adam first, but this simple fact does not mean that men are more important or more valuable than women; it is simply the order of creation that we find in the biblical text. The apostle Paul refers to this fact in 1 Timothy 2, so it has at least some importance for understanding the gender roles ordained by God. In Genesis 2:18–25, we see that God made Eve as a "helper" for Adam. The woman, then, was formed by God to be the perfect complement for the man. It is very clear that God took the literal flesh of Adam and used it to create Eve. Eve came "from" the "flesh" of Adam; she was made of the same stuff as he was. This allowed them to have a "one-flesh" relationship—marriage—that was a beautiful union between two beings made in God's likeness.

1. Describe the process of the creation of Eve by God. What need in Adam's life was identified as the reason for Eve's creation? How did Eve perfectly match Adam in their relationship?

2. What was Adam's reaction to Eve joining him in the garden of Eden?

3. What foundational aspects of male/female relationships are established in this passage?

THE FALL AND ITS CONSEQUENCES

Review pages 44–45 in *Tracing God's Story*

God placed Adam and Eve in the garden of Eden, where they lived with good work to do. They were also under the authority and rule of God's word. Adam and Eve were free to eat of every tree in the garden of Eden except for one: the tree of the knowledge of good and evil (Gen. 2:16–17). God promised that if they ate of that tree, they would die. If Adam and Eve continued in obedience to God's word, they would live forever in this beautiful place in close communion with their wonderful Creator.

But on a very sad day, Satan crept into God's good place and tempted Adam and Eve to sin. They chose freely to disobey God (Gen. 3:1–6). Adam and Eve *both* listened to the lies of Satan and ate the fruit of the tree of the knowledge of good and evil. They chose disobedience instead of obedience; death instead of life.

As the account of Genesis—and the rest of the Bible story—proves, sin really did enter the world on that day of the fall. It permeated all of creation through the disobedience of Adam and Eve. Immediately, Adam and Eve began to feel guilt and shame—emotions that they had never felt before. They recognized good and evil in a new way, and they became immediately closed off from God in their attitudes and actions. The rest of the Bible makes clear that through their sin, this world became a fallen place. Every human being is now born with a sin nature—a tendency toward sin that is natural, powerful, and unavoidable. Every single person tends toward sin and actually does sin. This is the devastating result of the fall. Because of this, all human beings—and the world itself—are now under God's wrath and judgment.

1. Describe what happened to God's word as both Satan and Eve interacted with it in Genesis 3. What did Satan try to do with God's word? How did Eve, in a different way, twist God's commands to his people? Why was this such a dangerous step to take?

2. What were the effects of the sin of Adam and Eve in the first moments following their disobedient choice (see Gen. 3:7)? Describe and explain their reaction.

---

3. From what you see in the world today, as well as in your own heart, what effect did this first sin seem to have—globally and throughout history? How then might you summarize what happened in Genesis 3 in theological terms?

OUT FROM EDEN

Review pages 47–50 in *Tracing God's Story*

A sad result of sin for God's people is that God drove them out of the perfect place he had made for them. Adam and Eve could no longer dwell in the garden of Eden in such close proximity to the holy God, for he cannot bear to be in the presence of sin. Genesis 3 ends with the man and the woman being sent away from God's place, with an angel guarding the entrance to the garden of Eden with a "flaming sword." The relationship between God and man had been forever damaged; only God would be able to make it right again.

1. How did God's curse for sin affect the woman (Gen. 3:16)?

_____

_____

2. How did God's curse for sin affect Adam (Gen. 3:17–19)?

_____

_____

_____

_____

3. What was the result of sin, for God's people, in relation to God's good place, the garden of Eden (Gen. 3:22–24)?

_____

_____

_____

_____

THE FIRST GOSPEL WORD

Review pages 51–52 in _Tracing God's Story_

In Genesis 3:15, God promised that one day the head of Satan—the serpent—would be "bruised" in a final way. Although Satan would "bruise [the] heel" of the one who would bruise (or "crush") his head, his own "injury" would be much more severe. The crushing of his head implies his death; he would not be able to survive such an injury! God promised that this victory over Satan would be achieved by a real "offspring" of Eve—that is, a literal human descendant. God was saying that someone would come—a human—who would gain a final victory over Satan, sin, and death. Because of this great promise from God, this verse has been understood by many to be pointing forward to Jesus's final victory over Satan and his gift of salvation for his people. Jesus is the one who came as the offspring of Eve—fully human and fully God—to crush the head of Satan through his death for sin on the cross and his victory over death through his resurrection from the grave. This first gospel word from

God was a promise about his own Son, who would one day come into the world to fix forever the mess that sin has created!

1. What exactly did God promise in this passage?

    ....

    ....

    ....

    ....

2. Why might theologians often refer to this verse as the protevangelium, or "first gospel" in the Bible?

    ....

    ....

    ....

    ....

3. What does this promise from God teach us about God himself and about his salvation plan for his people?

    ....

    ....

    ....

    ....

⬙ RECAP

In just the third chapter of the Bible, we read about the great crisis that erupted when Adam and Eve rejected God's good word and led all of creation into sin, fallenness, and corruption. Even so, the story was not over. God's first promise of gracious salvation came on the heels of the fall of Adam and Eve, reminding us that his plan for his people is good; he will not turn his back on his creation, despite sin and rebellion. The serpent crusher would come!

▼ SO WHAT?

As you conclude this chapter, jot down answers to the following application questions:

1. Explain why Genesis 1–3 is foundational for the rest of the Bible story. Why is it important for your own life to begin with the concept of God as Creator—the one who made you? How might that truth be the first step in sharing the gospel with someone?

----

2. List the key truths about God, the world, and human beings that emerge in these first chapters of the Bible, and explain why these truths are essential for understanding everything else that happens in the rest of the biblical story.

GOD'S PROMISE OF A PEOPLE
PART 1

Despite Adam and Eve's fall into sin—taking the whole human race with them—God did not abandon his creation but kept dwelling and working with his people. And he began to reveal his great salvation plan of blessing for the world.

SIN—HERE TO STAY

Review pages 56–60 in *Tracing God's Story*

Genesis 4 opens with the birth of two sons to Adam and Eve, who began to have children after they were cast out from the garden of Eden. Cain and Abel grew up together and began to make sacrifices—offerings—to their Creator God. For reasons that the text does not specify, God was pleased with the offering of Abel (who brought sheep to God as sacrifices) and not pleased with the offering of Cain (who brought some of his crops). Cain became angry and envious, and decided to do the unthinkable: he murdered his brother Abel in a field. To make matters worse, instead of repenting and crying out to God for mercy, he answered God with those chilling words that you probably know well: "Am I my brother's keeper?" (v. 9). Adam and Eve's sin had been passed down to their children. Cain and Abel had both entered the world with Adam and Eve's guilt hanging over them, but they also had a real "bent" toward sin, which meant that they necessarily *would* sin. This sad story shows us that sin had really entered the world to stay.

1. In what ways does Genesis 4 show us clearly the reality of the sin nature that was passed down from Adam and Eve to their children?

----

2. Describe the different elements of sin, rebellion, and hatred that show up in this chapter (make sure you look at the rest of the chapter, not only the account of Cain and Abel). How do you see evil and depravity taking over the world, even in these first generations?

GOD AND SIN

Review pages 59–61 in *Tracing God's Story*

We have been examining the way that sin and death spread into all the world—and all of humanity—in the years following the first sin of Adam and Eve in the garden of Eden. In Genesis 6, we see that this spread does not slow down as the story continues; if anything, it begins to accelerate. The sad summary of all of this is that "every intention of the thoughts of [man's] heart was only evil continually" (v. 5). The next verse even tells us that God "regretted" that he had made humanity. This does not mean, of course, that God did not have a plan for all of this. It is a way of putting God's reaction to sin in human language. God's "emotional" response to the sin of humanity was to be deeply grieved—and deeply angered—by all that was happening on earth.

1. What do we learn about God—particularly his attitude and response toward human sin—in Genesis 6?

-----

2. What is your immediate emotional reaction to this passage? What does this reaction tell you about your understanding of God's holiness, justice, and wrath against sin?

-----

3. What does the contrast of Noah with the rest of the world tell us about God's "favor," which is mentioned in this passage (Gen. 6:8)? What is the only hope for human beings who sin and live in a sinful world?

GOD'S JUST WRATH

Review pages 61–62 in *Tracing God's Story*

Genesis 7–8 gives us an account of the great flood that God brought upon the earth because of human sin. We must not miss the primary point of this account! If anyone tells you that the God of the Bible is only a God of grace (with no justice and wrath), they are mistaken. God is gracious, yes, but he is also infinitely holy. That means he cannot bear the presence of sin, which is opposed to his holy and righteous character. The flood was not the final judgment, because life on earth continued after it. But it was a picture of God's final judgment of the world, which is really coming one day. The holy God of the universe really will judge sin. Human sin and rebellion are so serious that God's response to it was to deluge the entire world with water in order to "blot out" (7:4) almost all of humanity. The ark was an incredible and vivid reminder, though, of God's grace amid his judgment. God could have wiped out Noah and his family as well, but he did not. Noah, who had found "favor" in God's eyes (6:8), was saved by God. In God's mercy, he also allowed for the animals to continue, as Noah brought them onto the ark as well.

1. What do you find hard to understand about this account? Is there anything that is difficult for you to accept? Explain.

2. What must be true about God, according to Genesis 7–8? What must be true about human beings, according to this passage?

3. What hope does this account point us toward?

GOD'S GREAT PROMISE

Review pages 63–66 in *Tracing God's Story*

In Genesis 11:27, we meet a very important biblical character—Abram. Genesis 12 begins with God calling Abram to leave his homeland and making very significant promises to him. The first aspect of the promises that God made to Abram was land. God sent Abram to a "land" (v. 1) that he promised to show him and later give to his descendants. Thus, central to God's promises to Abram was a new place where God's people would dwell. You remember, of course, that Adam and Eve were kicked out of the garden of Eden by God because of their sin. Now God was promising to bring this new people to a new place where he would reign over them again.

God also promised Abram that he would make a "great nation" out of him (Gen. 12:2). This was a strong promise of many descendants—a people that would come from Abram's line, and who would follow God and serve him in the land where they were going. God promised, in other words, to raise up from sinful humanity a group of people who would belong to him in a special way. Abram would be the first of these people.

Finally, as you probably noticed, God's words and promises were rich with the talk of "blessing" (Gen. 12:2–3). God promised not only to bless Abram but also to bless "all the families of the earth" through him. This was where the promise from God to Abram became really, really large. We might have expected God to promise blessing to Abram himself. But this blessing was going to be much bigger than one man only. God was saying that the blessing that he would pour out on this new people would have a global effect; it would bring blessing to everyone in the world everywhere. This was a huge promise that only God himself could make—and keep!

1. Describe the specific aspects of the promise that God made to Abram. Make sure that you capture each aspect of what God told him.

2. List all that we know about Abram before God called him in Genesis 12. Explain what this tells us about God's call to him.

3. What do we find out about Abram based on his response to the call of God?

ABRAM, MELCHIZEDEK, AND A COVENANT

Review pages 66–70 in *Tracing God's Story*

In Genesis 14:17–20, Abram encounters a mysterious figure named Melchizedek. Abram's strange interaction with this man has led some biblical scholars to conclude that Melchizedek (whose name, literally translated, means "king of righteousness," according to Hebrews 7:2) was Jesus Christ himself, appearing to Abram in a preincarnate (before the incarnation) form. This is certainly a possibility, but it seems better to understand him simply as a man whom God used to bless Abram and to point us forward to a later part of the big story of the Bible, when his own Son would enter the scene as the great, eternal Priest/King.

In Genesis 15, God makes a covenant with Abram. When the covenant ceremony was set up, *God himself* passed between the divided pieces of the animals! The "smoking fire pot" and the "flaming torch" (v. 17) were symbols of God's presence; he was the one who moved through the ceremony in the place usually reserved for the servant. As he did this, he reaffirmed his great promises to Abram, swearing to give the land that was laid out before him as the inheritance of his descendants.

What does this all mean? This account shows us that there were no conditions attached to God's covenant with Abram; it was unconditional. God had set his favor and blessing on this man, and he would carry out all the promises he had made to him. God swore this on his own life!

1. What do we learn about God as we read Genesis 15? In what ways did he reaffirm his promises to Abram in this part of the book of Genesis?

_____

_____

_____

_____

2. What was Abram's response to God's word in Genesis 15:6? What did God do for Abram in response to his belief?

_____

_____

_____

_____

3. Why might Genesis 15:6 be significant for the rest of the Bible story? What does this verse tell us about the way that human beings can find righteousness in the sight of God?

_____

_____

_____

_____

A COVENANT SIGN

Review pages 70–72 in _Tracing God's Story_

In Genesis 17, we see God, for the first time, establishing a covenant sign with Abraham and his people. He changed Abram's name to Abraham (v. 5), then asked Abraham for his obedience—not as a condition of his covenant but as a response to his great promise.

Remember, God had already "counted" Abraham as righteous because of his faith (15:6); his obedience could not now be the reason that God would be faithful to him. God commanded Abraham to take on himself—and on all the males that would be a part of his family and his people—the sign of circumcision (17:10). This would become a physical mark that would identify Abraham and the rest of God's people as truly belonging to God in a specific way.

1. Why did God change Abram's name to Abraham in the beginning of this passage?

2. What did God do, in Genesis 17:4–8, before calling Abraham to obey him and keep the covenant sign? Why is this important to see?

3. What was the specific sign that God gave to Abraham for his people, and what was this meant to signify?

◆ RECAP

God's insistent grace shines through this portion of the Bible story as he initiated promises to his people—promises to bless them, grow them, and work through them to extend his saving blessing to the nations of the world. God saved Noah and his family from the judgment of the flood, then swore by himself to make a people for his own glory from the family of Abraham. So the story continues!

▼ SO WHAT?

As you conclude this chapter, jot down answers to the following application questions:

1. What are several ways that you see God's *grace* emerging clearly through the accounts of Genesis 4–17?

2. Explain at least three or four ways that God's grace dominated how he interacted with his world and his people in the accounts that you have read and studied. What lessons do these examples of divine grace teach you as you seek to live for God?

Chapter 5

GOD'S PROMISE
OF A PEOPLE
PART 2

God had promised Abraham that he would give his descendants a land, that he would make those descendants numerous, and that he would bless those descendants and, through them, the world. Genesis 17 tells us how God began to fulfill those promises.

GOD KEEPS HIS PROMISES

Review pages 74–76 in *Tracing God's Story*

In Genesis 17:15 and the following verses, we learn that God came to Abraham and reaffirmed his promises to him very clearly. He even said, explicitly, that he was going to give Abraham a son *by Sarah*, Abraham's elderly wife (v. 16). Abraham's response, then, is surprising—and a bit disappointing. He cried out to God that he might bless "Ishmael" (v. 18). Ishmael was Abraham's son with Hagar—Sarah's servant. Abraham and Sarah had agreed on this action because both had begun to seriously doubt that Sarah could really have a child of her own in her old age. So Abraham's plea for God to bless Ishmael was a sign of Abraham's doubt. He did not think that God could give him a son through his aging wife; he decided to try to "help" God out a bit. However, God reaffirmed that Sarah would have a son (v. 19), and God's angels did the same (18:10), adding that Sarah would give birth in the next year! We see that despite Abraham and Sarah's doubts and struggles to believe, God remained faithful to his promise.

1. Why did Abraham reference Ishmael in his response to God? Who was Ishmael? Read back in Genesis 16 to get the full context for this part of the story.

2. Describe Abraham's response to God's promise in this passage. Does it seem that he struggled in believing God's word? Why or why not?

3. Describe Sarah's response as she heard God's promise (Gen. 18:12–14). How did God respond to this?

GOD TESTS ABRAHAM

Review pages 76–77 in *Tracing God's Story*

As he had promised, God enabled Sarah to bear a son for Abraham—Isaac (Gen. 21:1–7). But then, in Genesis 22, God gave Abraham a shocking command to test him. He told Abraham to take Isaac to the land of Moriah and offer him as a burnt offering. How did Abraham respond? Abraham took his beloved son and went to the place where God had told him to go. He tied Isaac up and prepared for the sacrifice. Just as he raised the knife to kill his son, however, God called out for him to stop. He told Abraham that he had seen that he loved him even more than his own son. God then provided a substitute sacrifice for Abraham's son—a ram that was caught by its horns in a nearby thicket. God was indeed testing Abraham to observe his loyalty and love for God first—even before his own son. The author of Hebrews later explains to us that Abraham, as he was preparing to sacrifice his son, had faith that God would raise Isaac from the dead if he went through with it (11:17–19). God was *not* like the deities and idols of the surrounding nations, demanding child sacrifice. At the climactic moment, God provided a substitute. In time, God would offer a sacrifice instead of demanding the lives of his people because of their sin.

1. If you were Abraham, what would have been your general attitude toward Isaac—this "child of the promise" that God had given to you?

2. Describe the human reactions that Abraham probably had to the command that God gave to him in Genesis 22.

3. What in this account might point us forward to God's future work in the world through Jesus Christ?

FROM ABRAHAM TO ISAAC

Review pages 78–79 in *Tracing God's Story*

In Genesis 24, Abraham made plans to find a wife for Isaac, but God sovereignly worked out the details. When Abraham's servant saw that God had led him to Abraham's relatives, it is no wonder that he cried out, "Blessed be the Lord, the God of my master Abraham, who has not forsaken his steadfast love and his faithfulness toward my master. As for me, the Lord has led me in the way to the house of my master's kinsmen" (v. 27). We cannot help but see, along with Abraham's servant, that God powerfully orchestrated the details of this meeting and provided the right wife for Isaac—the child of the promise. The overwhelming sense that we get from this chapter is that God's promise to Abraham—and to his descendants—would continue. He was not done working out all the details of the growth and blessing of Abraham's family; in fact, he was just getting started.

1. In what ways do you see evidence of God's hand in this account of Abraham's servant finding Rebekah?

---

2. What does all of this teach us about God's commitment to his promise to Abraham?

---

3. How can this chapter encourage us today, even when we do not obviously see God's hand at work in the world?

JACOB AND ESAU

Review pages 79–82 in *Tracing God's Story*

Jacob's name means "he takes by the heel." He got this name because he grabbed his twin brother Esau's heel during their birth. That action came to characterize his life, as he quickly proved to be a sneaky young man who did what he could to selfishly "grab" for himself what he wanted. First, he grabbed the birthright from Esau. Jacob caught Esau in a moment of weakness—so hungry that he would do and say practically anything to get some food. Jacob took advantage of this and forced Esau to sell him his birthright (the privileges and rights that belonged to the older son) for a bowl of stew. Esau, though, was not without fault in this transaction. He was shortsighted; he let his belly dictate what he wanted; and he thought only about the moment. Yet we are going to see that despite these far-from-perfect people, God's promise was going to continue.

1. Read Genesis 25:19–26. In what ways does the description of the birth of Jacob and Esau (their names, their physical characteristics, their actions, etc.) seem to establish their individual characters and the ways they will act?

-----

2. What does the account of Esau's sale of his birthright (vv. 29–34) tell you about Jacob? What does it tell you about Esau? What did all this mean for God's promise, which would be passed on from Abraham to Isaac and then to one of his sons?

GOD'S PURSUIT OF JACOB

Review pages 83–85 in *Tracing God's Story*

Later, Jacob also stole Esau's blessing by their father, Isaac (Gen. 27). After that, Esau was so angry that Jacob had to flee for his life to Haran, where he lived with his uncle, Laban (vv. 41–45). Through all his time with Laban, we do not get much information about the nature of Jacob's relationship with God. But we can suspect that he was beginning to change a bit in his heart. Perhaps getting a taste of his own medicine from Laban helped humble him a bit. Perhaps he began to turn in faith to the God of his grandfather, Abraham. We simply cannot be sure what was going on in Jacob's heart. We do know, though, that after Jacob finally left Laban with his family, God met him face to face. If you have time, read Genesis 32, which contains the account of Jacob wrestling with God in the middle of the night. In many ways, this struggle with God was typical of Jacob's entire life; he had repeatedly sinned and resisted obedience and faith in God. This time, though, Jacob wrestled with God and held onto him, demanding that God bless him. God did bless him, and he changed Jacob's name to "Israel," telling him that he had "prevailed" in his wrestling with God (v. 28). Jacob's nighttime wrestling match with God seems to have been a turning point for him, as he began to embrace God's promise and live as a man of faith in the God of his father and grandfather.

1. Where did you see Laban before in the Genesis story? What hint did you get back then about his character and motivations?

2. How did Laban give Jacob a taste of his own medicine? How might God have used this in Jacob's life and heart?

3. What did you learn about God's faithfulness to Jacob in this passage?

JACOB AND HIS SONS

Review pages 85–87 in *Tracing God's Story*

During his time in Haran while working for Laban, Jacob became the father of eleven sons (another was born later, during his return journey to Canaan). These sons of Jacob, as you probably know, would become the "fathers" of the twelve tribes of Israel—the people of God. It is becoming more and more obvious to us that the promise that God gave to Abraham was being passed down from generation to generation—from Abraham to Isaac and now to Jacob and his family. We know that this promise from God did not depend on the goodness of his people because we know about the many failures of Jacob before he ultimately put his faith in the God of his fathers. God was faithfully carrying out his work in the lives of his people from generation to generation; he was working to bring his saving blessing into the world through them.

In Genesis 37, we read that Joseph, Jacob's second-youngest son, had two dreams. In the first dream, his brothers' sheaves of wheat bowed down to his sheaf of wheat. In the second dream, the sun, the moon, and eleven stars bowed down to him. While Joseph probably should have kept quiet about these dreams, they were truly from God. Terrible things were going to happen to Joseph soon, but God was giving a hint of where this story was going to lead, as he would bring Joseph to a position of great power and authority in Egypt.

1. Read Genesis 37:3. Why might Jacob's favoritism toward Joseph have been a problem in his family? Where might Jacob have learned this?

2. What might Joseph's dreams have been pointing forward to? Why might it not have been wise for him to share them so boldly with his brothers and father?

3. What in this account is shocking or surprising to you?

JOSEPH'S FALL AND RISE

Review pages 87–91 in *Tracing God's Story*

Joseph's brothers were so angry about his dreams, they sold him into slavery in Egypt (Gen. 37:12–36). But in Genesis 39, we notice a repeated refrain, which the author of Genesis uses to remind us that God was active in every part of Joseph's life: "The LORD was with him" (vv. 2, 3, 21, 23). As a slave in Egypt, Joseph worked hard (and was blessed by God) to grow and prosper in the service of Potiphar. Then, just as things seemed to be getting better, he was falsely accused and thrown into prison. In Genesis 40–41, after many long years, God brought Joseph out of prison and into a place of unimagined authority and power in the land of Egypt—ruling at the right hand of Pharaoh himself!

All that God was doing—even through the evil actions of Joseph's brothers—was focused on bringing his people to Egypt so that they could be saved from death and starvation during a coming time of famine. Once there, they began to prosper, flourish, and explode in numbers for four hundred years. God's big promise to Abraham—of blessing through his people to all the nations—was being fulfilled in partial ways through this Joseph account. Joseph—a descendant of Abraham—became God's way of bringing blessing—rescue from famine—to people from all nations of the world.

1. What is a human perspective on these events that would have left Joseph completely discouraged and defeated (especially because of what happened to him in Gen. 39)?

---

2. What are some signs that you see in these chapters that point to the fact that Joseph had come to personally know and trust God?

---

3. In what ways do you finally see the big picture of God's work in Joseph's life coming together in these chapters? How do you begin to see his sovereignty in all that happened to Jacob?

⬙ RECAP

God's promise continued from generation to generation—from Abraham to Isaac to Jacob and through Jacob's son Joseph to the surrounding nations during the time of Pharaoh. Despite the hard and rebellious hearts of his people, God kept his promises. He was forming a family for himself, calling them to take him at his word and believe his gracious promises to them.

▼ SO WHAT?

As you conclude this chapter, jot down answers to the following application questions:

1. As you consider the life and account of Joseph, describe how you see the events of his life connecting to God's overarching work in the lives of his people. In other words, how did his individual experience connect to God's great plan and promise for his people? How can this experience of Joseph teach you about the connection between your individual "story" and God's big-picture work in the world? Why might belonging to a church, then, be so important for individual Christians?

GOD'S PEOPLE GROW
PART 1

After Joseph died, years and centuries went by, and Jacob's family grew into a great multitude of people, just as God had promised. But the Egyptian rulers became less and less comfortable with an ever-increasing number of Israelites in their midst. Pharaoh felt threatened by them and responded out of fear by making them all his slaves.

GROWING IN EGYPT

Review pages 93–96 in *Tracing God's Story*

The opening chapter of Exodus recounts Pharaoh's harsh treatment of the people of Israel. He set taskmasters over them and put them to work doing hard manual labor. Pharaoh was extremely cruel to them. We know, from later in the story, that God's people begin to cry out to him for help. Even though God's people had a serious problem, two very big hints of God's blessing emerge from this passage—first to his people and then to those who were not naturally his people. First, God's people continued to multiply, even under the oppression and cruelty of Pharaoh (Ex. 1:12). Pharaoh simply could not keep God's people down! Second, the midwives assisting Hebrew women refused to murder the male children of the Israelites as they had been commanded to do by Pharaoh. Their resistance honored God—and allowed God's people to continue growing.

1. Did you notice the especially ominous verse in this passage? In what ways does Exodus 1:8 warn us that something bad is coming for God's people?

-----

2. Which verses describe the way that God had richly kept his promises to Abraham?

-----

3. Where in this passage do you see signs of God's blessing coming to people who were not part of Israel? How might this be a sign of what is to come later in the Bible story?

A SPECIAL CHILD

Review pages 96–99 in *Tracing God's Story*

In Exodus 2, we read about the birth of Moses, his miraculous deliverance from Pharaoh's wrath, and his flight to Midian after he killed an Egyptian. Near the end of the chapter, there is a hint that this man, on whom God's hand had been so evident and obvious, would have a role to play in the lives of God's people in the years to come. Just after Moses settles in Midian, the author of Exodus tells us of the "groaning" of the people of Israel (v. 23) as they cried out to God for help and for rescue from slavery. God saw his people, and he knew that they needed help. We are left wondering if Moses might have something to do with the way that God will answer the cries and groaning of his people.

In a way, we cannot help but look at the truly miraculous birth narrative of Moses as pointing us forward to a far greater birth narrative. One day, many years later in God's great story, his own Son would enter the world as a baby boy, born to a young virgin named Mary, and he would grow up to be the great Savior and deliverer of God's people. In the story of Moses, God was showing us a pattern of how he planned to work in the lives of his people to bring his blessing and salvation to them. He would do it by providing a deliverer who would release them from slavery, bondage, and death.

1. What are some ways that God's hand is obvious in this story, even if seeming "coincidences" are not directly attributed to him?

---

2. How was Moses set by God's plan in a very special place? What might God have been intentionally doing?

---

3. Why might the author have inserted verses 23–25 into Exodus 2 right after the account of the birth of Moses? What might he have been trying to tell us?

_____

_____

MOSES CONFRONTS PHARAOH

Review pages 99–100 in _Tracing God's Story_

In time, God called Moses to go back to Egypt to confront Pharaoh and lead the people of Israel out of bondage. At the beginning of Moses's confrontation with Pharaoh (Ex. 5), he probably wished he had stayed in the land of Midian. Pharaoh essentially laughed in Moses's face and denied his request to release the people of Israel so that they could worship God in the wilderness. But the request seems to have made him angry, because he increased the burden of work on the Israelites, forcing them to gather the straw they needed to make bricks (straw was an important component of their mode of construction). Even the leaders of Israel were upset with Moses, and chapter 5 ends with Moses turning to God in what seems almost like anger and despair. It was not a promising beginning for Moses as the leader of God's people!

Pharaoh's response to Moses, and to God, was an indication of his hard and sinful heart. He would stubbornly refuse to release God's people from slavery (probably because the Egyptian economy had come to rely, in large part, on the slave labor of the Israelites). Yet God would have glory over Pharaoh; his work for his people, through Moses, was only beginning.

1. How confident did Moses seem to be in his ability to lead God's people and speak to Pharaoh on God's behalf? Answer this question by referencing specific aspects of Moses's response to God's call in Exodus 3.

_____

_____

_____

_____

2. How did God give Moses confidence to serve him and lead his people?

_____

_____

3. What was Pharaoh's response to Moses's initial request (Ex. 5)?

4. What was the response of the people of Israel to Moses? How might this have made Moses feel at this point?

GOD'S DELIVERANCE

Review pages 100–102 in *Tracing God's Story*

Pharaoh continued to refuse to let God's people go, so God brought judgment on Egypt in the form of ten plagues (Ex. 7–12). The final judgment that God brought on Egypt was by far the worst: he promised to send his angel to take the life of every firstborn child in the entire land. This was a vivid picture that God was giving to his people—and to all of Egypt: sin against the God of the universe ultimately results in death. Pharaoh was playing a very dangerous game with the Creator God, and he would now pay for his stubbornness with the loss of his firstborn son.

God's people, though, would have a way out from this final judgment. As God prepared to bring this plague, he instituted something called the "Passover"—a meal and a ceremony that would mark his people and place them safely under his special sign. This included a very detailed process that God asked his people to go through. God was carefully and intentionally reminding his people that they were to be set apart from the people in Egypt—set apart for worship of him, and therefore spared from his terrible judgment that was coming on the land. God intended the Passover to become a continual feast for his people so that they would always remember this day.

1. What does Exodus 11:9–10 tell you about God's role in the stubbornness of Pharaoh? What does it tell you about Pharaoh's real choice in all of this?

2. What seems to have been the central sign of the Passover for God's people? What was this sign pointing forward to in the Bible story?

3. What was the result of this final plague in the land of Egypt?

PHARAOH VS. GOD

Review pages 102–4 in *Tracing God's Story*

After the tenth plague, Pharaoh finally consented to let the Israelites go, and they made their way as a body toward the Red Sea. The Red Sea crossing was the completion of God's saving actions for his people. He had taken them out of Egypt, but Pharaoh quickly changed his mind about releasing the people (probably because he realized that his entire slave labor force was exiting his country). So Pharaoh chased God's people with his entire army, and caught up to them near the Red Sea. However, the Egyptians could not get near the people all night because God caused a great darkness to fall upon them. Even so, Moses and the people cried out to God for help. In the morning, God performed one of the greatest miracles in the history of the world for his people: he separated the Red Sea before them, and God's people began crossing on dry ground. As Pharaoh's forces followed them in, God (through Moses) brought the waters of the sea rushing back together after the Israelites had crossed over, and all the Egyptians were destroyed. God brought a great salvation to his people on this day—in miraculous fashion—and they were finally freed from slavery and set apart to be God's special people. This became a climactic saving event that Moses sang about. God's people would look back on it for centuries as a picture of God's mighty actions for them.

1. In what ways was the Red Sea event the completion of God's saving work on behalf of his people? How did this miracle finish God's great deliverance of them?

2. What hints do you see of the sin of God's people in Exodus 14 and 16? Why is this hard to believe? Why should we not be too quick to judge them?

GOD GIVES THE LAW

Review pages 104–6 in *Tracing God's Story*

In Exodus 19–20, we read the very important account of God's people finally gathering in the wilderness and receiving his good law, which came to them through Moses. God intended to save his people, deliver them from slavery, and bring them into his service by giving them the gift of living under his good word. The law was *never* intended to be the way for someone to "earn" favor with God in a saving way—or become part of his true people. We know this because God saved his people and delivered them from slavery in Egypt *before* he gave them the law!

What was the purpose of the law, then? God gave it to his people to guide them as they lived as his set-apart people under his good word. It was to instruct them how to live in the presence of their holy God, who is perfect in every way. Salvation with this God is always by faith, through his grace and mercy; we know this from Abraham, who was saved by God through faith long before this law ever was delivered to his descendants. In Exodus 19–20, God's people listened to him speak as he gave them his law.

1. What had God already done for his people, according to the previous chapters of Exodus that you have read? Why was that significant in light of what began to happen in Exodus 20?

2. What questions do you have about God's law—either its meaning for the Israelites or its role in our lives today?

GOD'S PEOPLE REBEL

Review pages 106–8 in *Tracing God's Story*

Exodus 32 is one of the saddest chapters in the Bible, for it tells us how the Israelites created and worshiped a golden calf. Moses was on Mount Sinai to meet with God and receive his law. He had been gone for days, and the people began to wonder what had happened to him. Moses's brother Aaron, seeking to please the people and keep them happy, invited them to donate their gold jewelry to him. He then melted it down and created a statue of a calf. Then he invited the people to worship this image as the "gods" who had brought them out of Egypt (v. 4). When Moses came down from the mountain, where the true God had been giving him his good word for his people, he found the people bowing down in worship before this golden cow! Obviously, God was angry at his people for this sinful idolatry. God is invisible, holy, and infinite; he could never be represented by an image like this. Punishment would come for God's people because they had sinned against him with their idolatry. Interestingly, though, God allowed Moses to play a kind of mediatorial role—standing between God and the people as he pleaded for God's mercy and forgiveness toward them. There would be judgment for this terrible sin, but Moses mediated for God's people and reminded God of his grace and mercy.

1. What is so striking and awful about the sin of Aaron and the people in this passage? List some ways that this sin was surprising and especially despicable.

2. What was God's response to this sin, and what role did Moses seem to play for the people in response to God's anger?

3. What do we learn about God's people from this passage? What do we learn about their need?

SINNING AND WANDERING

Review pages 108–10 in *Tracing God's Story*

In Numbers 13–14, we find out that sometime later, when God's people were on the cusp of entering the promised land, Moses sent twelve spies into the land to bring back a report about it and the people who lived there. The spies brought back a mixed report: they said it was a good land, but the people who lived there were strong. Only two men—Joshua and Caleb—gave a favorable report, but God's people listened to the bad report of the other ten spies. The people began weeping at this frightening report, and even wishing that they had "died in the land of Egypt" (14:2) rather than being brought into battle against such frightening opponents in the land of Canaan. Even when Joshua and Caleb tried to speak up for God and his purpose, the people would not listen; in fact, they tried to stone these faithful men! God's people were sinning in terrible ways. They were doubting God's word. They were failing to believe his promises. They were acting as if the peoples of the land were more powerful than their mighty and holy God.

God was not pleased with this response. He punished the people by prohibiting them from immediately entering the land. But we still see grace in God's response. He listened to Moses, who interceded for the people and begged God to forgive them and show mercy to them. Ultimately, the people's punishment for their sinful lack of faith was to wander in the wilderness for forty years, waiting to enter the promised land (Num. 14:34). The unbelieving older generation would die out, and God would bring the younger generation into the land. God would keep his promise to Abraham, but not yet.

1. What was it about the land—and the people of Canaan—that made most of the spies bring back an unfavorable report?

2. What does the response of the people to the unfavorable report tell you about their view of God and their understanding of his power and promise?

3. How was God's punishment just but also gracious?

◆ RECAP

What God had promised to Abraham about the growth of his descendants had begun to happen; Israel had grown in strength and numbers in Egypt and had been delivered from slavery by God's hand through his servant Moses. God had brought this people under the guidance of his word—only to see them rebel and falter in faith yet again. Yet even in the wilderness wanderings, God never forsook his gracious promises to his stubborn and sinful people.

▼ **SO WHAT?**

As you conclude this chapter, jot down answers to the following application questions:

1. Explain the ways that you have seen God's faithfulness to his people during the accounts of this chapter (list and describe at least three of these). Then give at least two examples of the stubborn and faithless hearts of God's people. How can these stories help you uncover stubborn and faithless tendencies in your own heart? How might you confess those tendencies to God?

Chapter 7

GOD'S PEOPLE GROW
PART 2

God punished his unfaithful people by condemning them to wander for forty years in the wilderness before entering the promised land. The older generation would die during those years. Surprisingly, even Moses would die before the people entered the land.

FROM MOSES TO JOSHUA

Review pages 114–18 in *Tracing God's Story*

When God called and commissioned Joshua to lead the people of Israel after Moses, he reaffirmed his promise about the land to Joshua. Also, he commanded Joshua several times to be "strong and courageous" as he led God's people into Canaan, the land that had been promised to them according to God's word. Joshua had long been a great man of faith, and now he was the one whom God had chosen to succeed Moses in leading his people.

After Joshua was commissioned (Josh. 1), he immediately began preparing the people and letting them know that the conquest would soon begin. He reminded them of God's promises to them and encouraged them with the words that God had given him. Unlike the older generation (which had died out in the wilderness), this new generation responded with faith and commitment, swearing allegiance to Joshua and preparing to follow him into the land. This was a bright new day for the people of God.

1. How was Joshua supposed to lead God's people in relation to the word—the law—of God? Why would this be a key part of his leadership over the people?

---

2. What do you notice about Joshua's leadership from the first part of Joshua 1?

---

3. Read Joshua 5:13–15. What does this passage tell you about Joshua? How might this account point us forward in the Bible story to Jesus Christ?

ENTERING THE LAND

Review pages 118–19 in *Tracing God's Story*

In Joshua 6, we see how God gave the Israelites their first great victory in the promised land. The capture of Jericho shows us—again—God's commitment to faithfully keeping his promises to his people. After subjecting his rebellious people to forty years of wandering in the desert, God was still going to keep the promise that he had made so many years earlier to Abraham. He was going to take his people into Canaan. He was going to give them this land as their inheritance. He was going to bless them there and prepare them to be a blessing to all peoples of the earth. Also, this victory—especially the nature of this victory—was meant to remind God's people that *he* is the mighty warrior, the one who would do battle on their behalf. While God's people did eventually do some fighting as they entered the city, God chose to give his people a victory in such a fashion that they had no choice but to acknowledge that he was the only one responsible! The Israelites did not make the walls fall; it was God's miraculous power that did this.

1. If you had been in Joshua's place, how might you have been tempted to respond to God's instructions for the battle of Jericho? Why might these instructions have seemed strange? What was God asking Joshua—and his people—to do as they listened to his word?

2. What was the nature of the victory over Jericho meant to teach God's people? Why might God have chosen to conquer the city in this particular way?

THE CALL TO CONQUEST

Review pages 119–21 in *Tracing God's Story*

In Joshua 23–24, Joshua was nearing the end of his life. Sadly, the Israelites had not fully completed the conquest of Canaan under his leadership. In his final words to the people, Joshua commanded them to keep pressing forward. In his speech, he made clear that God's call to conquest in the promised land was ultimately about the purity of their worship. God's motivation as his people entered the land was for them to establish right worship of him—obedience to his word, unhindered by idolatry and the sinful practices of the peoples of the land. God wanted his people to be purified—set apart—for him and for right worship of him. That was—and is—God's good goal for his people.

Sadly, after Joshua died, the conquest—even though it was commanded by both Joshua and God—was not fully completed. We see this clearly in the book of Judges, which begins with the account of God's people failing to fully drive out the peoples of the land. As you can imagine, disastrous results came from this failure.

The book of Joshua, though, ends on a high note. God's people had become a great nation, and they were now in the land that God has promised to Abraham many years earlier. They seemed poised to live under God's blessing and to be a blessing to the peoples of the earth.

1. How did Joshua encourage the people of Israel to keep pushing forward in their conquest of the land?

2. What promises that God had made did Joshua affirm to the people?

3. What seems to have been the reason for God's command for the Israelites to drive out the peoples of the land? What did God seem to want from his people in all of this?

THE JUDGES CYCLE

Review pages 122–23 in *Tracing God's Story*

The book of Judges clearly shows us God's grace; he would not finally and permanently abandon his people and his plan for them even though they continually turned away from him into sin and rebellion. God kept raising up judges who got them out of trouble with their enemies. The book of Judges, though, also shows us clearly that God's people needed a permanent and godly king who could lead them in right worship of God in a lasting way. During the time of the judges, God's people were tied together loosely as a nation and were living in the land that God had promised them. But they were not living well under God's blessing, and they certainly were not bringing blessing to the nations around them.

1. Read Judges 2:6–3:6. Explain what you find in this passage regarding the people's obedience to the call of Joshua regarding the full conquest of the land.

2. What were the results of the people's actions regarding this conquest?

3. Explain how you understand the function of the judges during this time after Joshua's death. How were they a gift from God? How were they not a final solution to the people's sin problem?

GIDEON AND SAMSON

Review pages 123–27 in *Tracing God's Story*

Gideon and Samson were two of the most famous of the judges (Judg. 6–7, 13–16). Despite all of Gideon's weaknesses and doubts, God chose to use him to deliver his people from the Midianites. The people had called out to God for help, and he provided a very unlikely hero for them. God used Gideon—a weak and fearful man—to deliver his people. Afterward, God sent Samson and used him in mighty and powerful ways, but Samson himself was much like the rest of God's people during this time. He was constantly turning toward sin even as God continued to work powerfully in and through his life. Samson was a judge who resembled the people that he led. God's people still looked for a greater deliverer yet to come.

1. What about Gideon's response to God tells you that he was not a courageous and strong leader for God's people like Joshua?

----

2. What were some of the ways in which God used Samson powerfully for his people?

----

3. How might Samson point to the ministry of Christ for God's people?

....

....

RUTH

Review pages 127–31 in *Tracing God's Story*

The author of Ruth goes out of his way to keep reminding us that Ruth was a Moabite. In other words, she was not part of the people of Israel; she was a Gentile. Yet God showed favor to this Gentile woman, who turned in faith to him and wanted to be a part of his people. Because of Ruth's faith, she was brought into God's people. Even in the time of the judges, we see a fulfillment of God's promise to Abraham that "all peoples of the earth" would be blessed through him.

At the conclusion of the story of Ruth, we learn what God was doing through all of these events. God had been sovereignly orchestrating a marriage that would lead to the birth of the man who would one day be a good and faithful king over his people: David. Ruth married Boaz, who became the father of Obed, who became the father of Jesse, who became the father of David. Ruth, the Moabite who put her faith in God became the great-grandmother of King David.

1. What is the setting for the story of Ruth as the book begins? Why is this significant for the events of this story?

....

....

....

....

2. How did Boaz show himself to be a worthy man? Why was this striking and surprising, given the context?

....

....

....

....

3. How does the ending of this story show us the big picture of what God was doing through Ruth in the lives of his people?

_____

_____

_____

_____

⬥ RECAP

God's servant Joshua led the next generation of God's people into the promised land, fulfilling many of God's promises to Abraham. After Joshua, though, the period of the judges of Israel shows us again the stubborn, sinful, and idolatrous hearts of God's people. God had been faithful to them, but they remained not fully faithful to him. The events of the time of the judges show us that God's people needed a good and faithful king to rule over them and help them believe and obey God's word.

⬇ SO WHAT?

As you conclude this chapter, jot down answers to the following application questions:

1. Explain the Judges cycle, step by step, as if you were explaining it to someone who is not very familiar with the Bible. Give the context for this cycle and explain to this person what this cycle teaches us about human nature and about the Israelites' need for a Savior and King. Can you apply these conclusions to your own situation?

_____

_____

_____

_____

Chapter 8

GOD'S KINGDOM— RISE AND FALL
PART 1

Following the growth of God's people and their conquest of the promised land, the next major development in the Bible's big story is the founding of Israel's much-needed monarchy. As we think about this important part of the story, we'll look into the biblical books of 1 Samuel through 2 Chronicles.

SAMUEL: PROPHET, PRIEST, AND JUDGE

Review pages 133–38 in *Tracing God's Story*

Before Israel's first king was crowned, God's people were led by a great and godly man named Samuel. You can read about his birth and the start of his ministry in 1 Samuel 1 and 3. Samuel was a *priest*; that means he mediated the relationship between God and his people by helping the people worship God rightly through sacrifices and obedience. Samuel also was a *prophet*; he faithfully brought God's word to God's people in a powerful way as he led them. He also was the last and greatest *judge*, as he ruled God's people in a kind of "political" way (they all followed him). This means Samuel was a transitional figure between the period of the judges and the time of the monarchy in Israel. Samuel's fulfillment of these roles for God's people—priest, prophet, and judge/king—points ahead to the way that Jesus fulfilled the same roles perfectly.

1. Where did Samuel grow up? Why was that significant for the role that he would play for God's people?

_____

_____

_____

_____

2. How did Samuel function as a judge (a kingly figure) for God's people?

_____

_____

_____

_____

3. How did Samuel function as a prophet (one who brought God's word to God's people)?

_____

_____

_____

_____

4. How did Samuel function as a priest (one who mediated between God and the people and led in right worship)?

_____

_____

_____

_____

MEETING KING SAUL

Review pages 139–40 in *Tracing God's Story*

In 1 Samuel 8–9, we learn that the people of Israel asked Samuel to give them a king so they could be like all the other nations. It seems they were looking for a figurehead—someone whom they could admire and who would look the part of a king—and they found it in Saul. Chapter 9 begins by telling us that he was more handsome than anyone in Israel; he even stood head and shoulders above everyone in height. Saul was exactly what the people envisioned for a king who would lead them and fight their battles for them.

In 1 Samuel 11, we see that Saul had a very promising beginning to his reign. He won a great victory over the Ammonites, who were oppressing the people of Jabesh-gilead. Saul, it seemed, would be a great military leader.

We can imagine that God's people were excited about their new leader. The monarchy was beginning, and the nation of Israel was ready to grow and become strong. But would this promising beginning last? Would Saul be the king that the people were waiting for?

1. What was sinful about the people's request for a king? Where do you see their true motivation in their words?

2. How is Saul described, and what do you think the author of 1 Samuel may have been trying to tell us through this description?

3. Why might God's people have been very excited and optimistic as the reign of Saul began?

_____

_____

_____

_____

SAUL'S FAILURE

Review pages 140–43 in _Tracing God's Story_

Sadly, Saul's reign fell into a downward spiral almost from the start. In 1 Samuel 13, we read that Saul, during battle preparations, became impatient with Samuel, who had asked Saul to wait to make a sacrifice until he, the priest, was there to lead it. This would be in accordance with God's law. Saul, though, did something terrible—something that was against all the instructions of God. When Samuel did not show up quite on time, Saul conducted the sacrifice himself. He failed to obey the word of Samuel, and therefore of God. Then, in 1 Samuel 15, we see a different situation, but a very similar result. As Saul went into battle against the Amalekites—an ancient enemy of God and his people—he was given a very specific command from God: destroy _everything_. God's command was his way of bringing his righteous judgment against these violent and idolatrous people through his king, whom he had placed over his people. But again, Saul disobeyed the clear command of God. He left the best of the captured animals alive after his victory. As a result, Samuel told Saul that the kingdom would be ripped from his hand and given to another man.

1. In 1 Samuel 13, given the fact that Samuel had asked Saul to wait for him to lead the sacrifice, what was the specific sin of Saul? What did this sin demonstrate about his heart?

_____

_____

_____

_____

2. In 1 Samuel 15, what was the specific command of God that Saul received as he prepared for battle against the Amalekites? Explain his actions. What did this sin show about his heart?

3. Also in chapter 15, look at all of the different ways that Saul reacted to his sin and explain how these reactions demonstrated a heart that was not completely given over to God in worship.

DAVID: A MAN AFTER GOD'S OWN HEART

Review pages 143–45 in *Tracing God's Story*

The identification of David as the next king was almost totally different than the way Saul was chosen. Saul, remember, looked the part in every way. He was handsome, tall, and strong—just like a king *should* look. David, though, wasn't even the most impressive person in his own house. One by one, Jesse brought his sons before Samuel, who was impressed by the looks of David's older brothers (even Samuel, it seems, was somewhat focused on outward appearances, at least at first). Finally, though, the youngest brother—David, the shepherd boy—was called in from the fields. Samuel anointed David as the next king after God assured Samuel that "the LORD looks at the heart" (1 Sam. 16:7). It was this young, unexpected, man who had the heart that God desired for the king who would rule his people. God soon demonstrated that he was indeed with this young man, as he gave David a mighty victory over the giant Goliath, delivering his people from defeat.

1. In what ways was David an unexpected choice to be the next king of Israel? How did he surprise even Samuel as the one God chose?

_____

_____

_____

_____

2. How did God use David—almost immediately—to begin delivering his people?

_____

_____

_____

_____

3. How does 1 Samuel 16–17 point us forward to Jesus's anointing by God and his role in the lives of God's people?

_____

_____

_____

_____

GOD'S COVENANT WITH DAVID

Review pages 145–46 in _Tracing God's Story_

In 2 Samuel 7, God made a massive promise to David. When David wanted to build a house, or temple, for God, God instead promised to build a "house" for him. This house, according to God, would be a royal line that would continue _forever_. We need to understand how massive this promise was. This "Davidic covenant" was a promise that long after David's death, a literal "Son of David" would rule over God's people forever. It was a promise of a "forever kingdom" with a "forever king." It is no wonder that David responded to this promise of God with humble praise and worship. He could not believe the favor that God had shown to him, and he prayed to God with gratitude and joy. That should be our reaction, too, for this promise still holds today. God is keeping this promise to his people through the reign of King Jesus, Son of David.

1. What motivated David to build God a house in Jerusalem? Why did God ultimately refuse this offer from David?

2. What did God promise David in this chapter? Why was this promise so big? In what way could this promise actually be fulfilled?

3. What was David's response when he heard God's great promise to him?

DAVID'S FAILURE AND REPENTANCE

Review pages 145–50 in *Tracing God's Story*

2 Samuel 11–12 recounts David's terrible fall into sin. After he lusted for and then committed adultery with Bathsheba, he arranged for Bathsheba's husband to be put to death.

After Uriah was killed, David took Bathsheba as his own wife. Chapter 11 ends with an ominous statement: "The thing that David had done displeased the LORD" (v. 27). For a while, David seemed to go on with life as usual, with Bathsheba as his new wife. It took God's word, through the prophet Nathan, to convict David for his sin and wake him up to the reality of what he had done.

Psalm 51 shows us a king who, although far from perfect, really was a man after God's heart. He cried out to God for mercy and grace, and he found it by faith. We know from the big story of the Bible that this prayer of David for grace from God was fully answered through the death of the great Son of David, Jesus, who died for King David's sins on the cross too!

1. How does one sin lead to many more sins in this passage? What does this teach us about sin?

....

....

....

2. How did Nathan the prophet show David the seriousness of his sin?

....

....

....

3. In Psalm 51, in what ways did David ask God to get to the root of his sin and change his heart?

....

....

....

◈ **RECAP**

As Samuel anointed Saul (who failed) and then David (a man after God's own heart), we see many of God's promises to Abraham partly fulfilled. God's people were in the land, gathered under God's word, and under the rule of a godly king. Even so, David's failures remind us that he was sinful and fallen—just like God's people. We begin to look beyond David to a forever king and an eternal kingdom.

▼ **SO WHAT?**

As you conclude this chapter, jot down answers to the following application questions:

1. Describe the differences between Saul and David given their sin, their response to their sin, and God's rejection of Saul and acceptance of David. What seems to have set these two men apart? How can you learn from David in your response to your own sin?

2. How do the lives of both Saul and David point us forward to the need for a better Savior and King for God's people? Why should these stories increase your love and admiration for Jesus?

Chapter 9

GOD'S KINGDOM— RISE AND FALL
PART 2

In time, David's son Solomon was born. He would inherit the throne of Israel after his father and would take Israel to even greater heights than it experienced during David's reign. It's not hard to imagine that God's people during this time wondered if Solomon might be the eternal King they needed.

AFTER KING DAVID

Review pages 154–55 in *Tracing God's Story*

David had wanted to build a temple for God, but God gave that task to Solomon, David's son and heir to the throne. Solomon dedicated great resources to this place for the worship of God by his people. In 1 Kings 7–8, we read about the fine materials that went into its construction; still, it was not quite so big and glorious as Solomon's palace. We also notice that Solomon prayed a great prayer to God as the temple was dedicated to him for worship. Solomon asked God to keep his great promise to David as this temple was inaugurated. Second Chronicles 7, another version of this account, tells us that God's presence powerfully came down and dwelt in the temple; God chose to meet with his people in this place in a powerful way. We know that this temple became the primary place for God's people to meet with their God. Blood sacrifices were given for sin in this place, and God allowed sinful people to draw near to him in worship there. This physical temple would not stand forever, but its construction was a great moment in the history of the people of Israel, for it pointed to a much greater meeting place between God and man at the cross of Jesus Christ.

1. Do you see any hints in this passage about some heart problems that Solomon may have had?

----

2. How was God's blessing poured out on his people in a new way in this part of the Bible story?

----

3. What did the temple represent for God's people? How did God promise to act toward them in relation to this temple?

THE BLESSING OF GOD UNDER SOLOMON

Review pages 155–57 in *Tracing God's Story*

In 1 Kings 10:1–13—a passage that is probably the high point of the entire Old Testament—we see the blessing of God on his people spreading to all the peoples of the earth.

God's people—and God's king—were finally poised to become a blessing to all nations. As an example of this, the queen of Sheba (a great monarch from another nation) came to Jerusalem to see and experience the wisdom and the blessing of God there. She had heard of Solomon's incredible wealth and wisdom. As she tested him with difficult questions and saw every part of his kingdom, she was amazed; the text tells us that her experience took her breath away. Sadly, the heights of the kingdom of Israel—this brief and glorious moment of blessing through God's people and God's king to the nations of the earth—would not last very long.

1. In what ways do you see God's promises to Abraham being fulfilled in new ways in this passage?

2. How do you see God's blessing being shown to the nations in the events of this passage?

3. Why might we call this account the high point of the Old Testament?

SOLOMON'S DOWNFALL

Review pages 157–59 in *Tracing God's Story*

In 1 Kings 10:14–11:13, we read the sad account of Solomon beginning a downward trend into sin. In Deuteronomy 17, God had looked ahead to this day of kingship for his people through the leadership of Moses. He had given commandments for the kings who eventually would rule his people—commandments that would keep them dependent on him as the true King of the people (by not getting too rich or relying too much on military power) and that would keep them worshiping him as the true God of the people (by not taking many wives, who might turn their hearts toward idolatry). Solomon, at the very height of his kingship and the high point of the Old Testament, began to break God's commandments one by one as the king of God's people. We will see that even Solomon—the great son of David who built the glorious temple for the worship of God—was not the final and perfect King that God's people needed. There was to be someone even greater than Solomon— someone who would be not just great for a while, but perfect. That King would be able to lead God's people in a forever kingdom, where there would be no more sin, idolatry, or death at all.

1. What specific sins did Solomon fall into during his reign, according to this passage?

2. How do you know that these activities and pursuits were sinful?

3. What results did these activities and pursuits seem to have on his life and heart?

A DIVIDED KINGDOM

Review pages 159–60 in *Tracing God's Story*

Just one generation after Solomon, the kingdom of Israel split into two parts—never to be fully joined again. In 1 Kings 11:9–12:33, we see that after Solomon's son Rehoboam became king, he listened to unwise counsel and treated the people harshly. As a result, ten of the twelve tribes of Israel (all except for Judah and Benjamin) decided to follow a far more evil man—Jeroboam—instead of Rehoboam. They broke away from the rule of Rehoboam and the centrality of Jerusalem to form the northern kingdom: Israel. The two remaining tribes were thereafter referred to as the southern kingdom: Judah. Only God stepping in prevented a full-blown civil war over this split, although that would happen later in the story. This was a very sad day for God's people—just one generation removed from the heights of Solomon's reign.

Sadly, Jeroboam was a far worse leader than even the foolish Rehoboam. The people of Israel began bowing down to statues of calves instead of worshiping the one true God. The northern kingdom would never have a fully good king. Judah would have a few more righteous kings, but even they began to head downhill into sin and idolatry. The kingdom had been divided, and the downward slope toward punishment and exile had begun.

1. What was gracious about God's response to Solomon's sin? What was just about God's response?

----

2. What was so foolish about Rehoboam's early decisions as the king of Israel?

---

3. What was the result of Rehoboam's folly as the leader of God's people? What began to happen in Israel under the rule of Jeroboam?

THE DOWNWARD SPIRAL OF THE KINGDOMS

Review pages 160–65 in *Tracing God's Story*

In 1 Kings 15:9–16:6, we see that, in general, the kings who ruled over the northern kingdom—Israel—were evil, idolatrous, and disobedient to God. Even though some of them showed moments of goodness and repentance, the kings of Israel generally led God's people into depths of sin and idolatry that had never been known in the kingdom before. Nadab and Baasha are good examples of this. Nadab "walked in the way of his father" (15:26), Jeroboam, and led Israel into more sin and idolatry. Baasha, after killing Nadab and taking the throne for himself, also did evil in God's eyes and led all of Israel into sin. We also see something that is demonstrated for us through the story of Baasha: the northern kingdom was a place of political unrest. Nadab's takeover was not the only time that someone grabbed power through a rebellion that ended in the murder of the seated king. Evil abounded, and many kings came to power through force. Judah, though, was a different story. There were sinful kings, of course, and Judah eventually followed Israel into idolatry and then exile. Still, there were kings in Judah who followed the path of David and sought to restore right worship to God's people as they obeyed his word. Asa was one of those kings; he "did what was right in the eyes of the LORD" (15:11).

1. What do you observe about Asa's reign? How was he a faithful and righteous king for God's people? How was he not a perfect king?

2. What do you observe about Nadab and then about Baasha? How did Baasha take over the throne of Israel? What were the characteristics of his reign?

HOSEA AND ELIJAH

Review pages 165–69 in *Tracing God's Story*

How did God respond to the sin of his people before the judgment of exile? He did not judge them without warning. Instead, he faithfully spoke to his people through prophets—men whom he began to raise up for his people during the time of the monarchy. Hosea is one example of a preexilic prophet. Hosea spoke to the northern kingdom—Israel—and was focused mainly on identifying and highlighting the adulterous and awful nature of its sin of idolatry. Specifically, Hosea went after the worship of Baal, which had become very prevalent in Israel (Hos. 1–2). Elijah, a nonwriting prophet who ministered in Israel during the time of King Ahab, was one of the greatest prophets in all of Scripture. In fact, John the Baptist was compared to—and identified with—Elijah when he came to bear witness to the coming of Jesus Christ as the New Testament began. Life was not easy for a prophet of God during the time of Ahab. Still, God worked mightily through Elijah, bringing about a great victory over the prophets of Baal and his servants (1 Kings 18).

1. How did Hosea's call from God (in his marriage) serve as a picture for God's people of their sin against him?

2. What sign did God do through Elijah to begin to send his word and his conviction to Ahab and the people of Israel (look back to 1 Kings 17–18)?

3. What lessons do we learn about God from these passages? What does he seem to be communicating to his people about himself?

THE EXILE

Review pages 169–71 in *Tracing God's Story*

After many years of warning his people through his prophets, God finally brought the judgment of exile on both Israel and Judah because of their sin. Israel went into exile first—to Assyria—in around 722 BC (see 2 Kings 15:29). God brought the mighty Assyrian army against the northern kingdom, over which no truly righteous kings had reigned. The people went away into slavery and never really returned—at least not all at once—to a unified kingdom in Israel. The existence of the ten tribes that composed the kingdom of Israel (the other two tribes, Judah and Benjamin, made up the kingdom of Judah) was all but destroyed through this exile. God's judgment—about which many of his prophets had warned for many years—had finally come to the northern kingdom.

Judah held out longer; God was patient with the southern kingdom, as there were some faithful and righteous kings (such as Josiah and Hezekiah, just to name a couple) who led God's people in reforms and in great returns to faithful worship. Still, Judah also declined steadily into more and more sin. Eventually, as we read in 2 Chronicles 36, its people also were conquered, captured, and taken away as slaves to Babylon (in roughly 586 BC).

1. How does 2 Chronicles 36 show us God's just judgment against the sin of his people?

2. In 2 Chronicles 36, what do you notice about the response of King Zedekiah to God's word, which came to him through the prophet Jeremiah?

3. How does 2 Chronicles 36:15–16 summarize and wrap up this period of history for God's people?

◇ **RECAP**

David's failures amid a generally faithful reign gave way to Solomon's greater failures (despite his great, God-given strength, wealth, and wisdom). The kingdom was divided and God's people never again experienced the blessings of the days of David and Solomon. The northern kingdom of Israel spiraled into sin and idolatry (and went into exile first), and the southern kingdom of Judah (despite some good and faithful kings) soon followed. God's people became slaves in foreign lands—and yet, God still did not abandon his gracious saving promises to them.

▼ **SO WHAT?**

As you conclude this chapter, jot down answers to the following application questions:

1. Discuss the ways that the reign of Solomon, with all its glory and blessing, can point us forward to the eternal reign of Christ Jesus over God's people. How can this account expose the fleeting nature of earthly pomp, wealth, and splendor—and remind you to find your treasure in heaven, with Christ?

2. Discuss the obvious ways in which King Solomon fell far short of being a perfect king for God's people. What warning does his fall provide for you?

GOD'S PEOPLE— CAPTIVE AND COMING HOME
PART 1

The sin of the people of Israel and Judah, especially their idolatry, led God to allow them to be captured and deported to other countries. There is much that is important for us to know about this period in the big story of the Bible.

FAR FROM HOME

Review pages 172–75 in *Tracing God's Story*

God had warned his people many times about their sin, especially idolatry, which their kings had led them to practice. Judah's King Zedekiah was the final ruler who rebelled against God; he rejected the word of God from Jeremiah, and God finally allowed the southern kingdom to be conquered. So God's purpose for the exile was to punish his people. But even this seventy-year time of captivity was not the end of the story. God was not done with his people.

Several biblical books help us understand what exile was like for God's people, while others record events of the return. The books of Daniel and Esther give us glimpses of God's faithfulness to his people during the general period of the exile. The two central books in the Bible that tell us about the return from exile to Jerusalem are Ezra and Nehemiah—books that are both named for their central human figures.

1. How has God already fulfilled his great promises to Abraham, at least in some ways, at this point in the Bible story?

_____

_____

_____

_____

2. How are we still waiting for God to fulfill his promises from Genesis 3:15 and from 2 Samuel 7 (check those references if you need to)?

_____

_____

_____

_____

DANIEL AND ESTHER

Review pages 175–79 in *Tracing God's Story*

In Daniel 1–2, we find the account of Daniel being taken away from the land of Israel with other captives. The narrative then moves quickly to the court and palace of the Babylonian king, where Daniel and other promising young Jewish men were gathered to serve King Nebuchadnezzar. It is already clear that God's work in Daniel's life was not done, as he received this great honor from the king of this pagan country. Like Joseph, Daniel was given great wisdom from God—wisdom to interpret dreams. Daniel interpreted the dream of Nebuchadnezzar—something that the wisest men of Babylon failed to do. By God's strength and hand, Daniel was exalted to an incredibly high position in Babylon.

In the book of Esther, we read that during the days of King Ahasuerus of Persia, Esther, a young Jewish woman (who had kept her ethnicity hidden), miraculously rose to the position of queen through a kind of ancient beauty contest. Then a man named Haman hatched a plot to destroy all the Jews living in the kingdom. Esther's uncle, Mordecai, hearing of the threat against the Jewish people, urged her to confront the king—her husband—and beg him for the lives of the Jewish people. Despite fearing for her life, Esther finally agreed to do this, Haman was exposed as a villain, and the Jewish people gained a tremendous victory over their enemies. They ended up much better off than before the threat from Haman began.

1. How did Daniel take a stand for God and for being set apart for him? How did God richly bless Daniel for this?

2. What did God seem to be showing to his people through his faithfulness to Daniel?

3. How did God use Esther to preserve the lives of his people? In what way did God not only preserve them but also make them even more prosperous than before?

EZRA AND THE TEMPLE

Review pages 179–82 in *Tracing God's Story*

Ezra 1–2 gives us an account of the first wave of exiles who came back from Babylon to Jerusalem. Ezra begins by pointing out to his readers that everything that happened to bring about the return of God's people was according to "the word of the Lord by the mouth of Jeremiah" (1:1). According to Ezra, God was keeping this word. Perhaps the most amazing part of this account is the way that God worked in the heart of a mighty pagan king—Cyrus—to decree this return to the land for his people. Cyrus, the king of the known world during this time, was only a pawn in the hands of God, who was working out his good purposes in the lives of his people. God stirred up this pagan king's heart to do exactly what he wanted him to do.

In Ezra 3, we are told that the returned exiles set to work rebuilding the temple. But even though this was a moment of great hope for God's people, the glory of the Lord did not descend on this temple the way it did on Solomon's temple (2 Chron. 5:13). It seems that God's presence might not have dwelt in this second temple in the same special way that it did in the first temple many years before. The old men wept as they realized that this new temple would never come close to comparing to the glories of the old temple; they could tell this just by looking at the foundation (Ezra 3:12). In short, Israel would not return to its former glory.

1. What did Ezra say about God's role in the decree that Cyrus, king of Persia, made regarding God's people? What does this remind us about God?

2. In what ways does Ezra 1–2 show God restoring his people?

3. What is the unexpected sadness of this passage (Ezra 3:12–13)? How does that sadness point us to Jesus Christ and his coming as a greater fulfillment of the hope of the temple?

EZRA THE SCRIBE

Review pages 182–84 in *Tracing God's Story*

About fifty years after the first exiles returned to Jerusalem, Ezra himself arrived to teach God's word to God's people. Ezra 7:10 is a remarkable summary of Ezra's commitments as a word-centered leader of the people. He was a man who had given himself to the careful study of God's word; his goal was to *know* it well. He also had devoted himself to doing what the word of God said; his goal was to *obey* everything that God had commanded. Finally, this verse tells us that Ezra had set his heart to make known the statutes of God to the people of Israel; his goal was to *teach* God's word faithfully to God's people. Ezra, then, was a great gift from God to his people during these days. He entered the story of God's people as a new faithful leader—a man who would call God's people back to right worship and obedience according to the word of God.

1. What do you observe from Ezra 7 about Ezra's commitments to God's word and to God's people?

2. Read Ezra 9–10. What was the big problem that Ezra found with God's people when he returned to Jerusalem?

....

....

....

....

3. How did God's people respond to the conviction that came upon them because of their sin after Ezra preached to them?

....

....

....

....

NEHEMIAH AND THE RESTORATION

Review pages 184–88 in *Tracing God's Story*

Along with Ezra, Nehemiah also played a major role in the lives of God's people during the time of the return from exile. According to Nehemiah 1–2, as Nehemiah was serving the Persian king, he received word that the walls of Jerusalem and the city in general remained in ruins—completely open to the attacks of any of the surrounding nations. By God's grace, the king allowed Nehemiah to return to Jerusalem to oversee the repairs of the city and its walls. Nehemiah, as we see from this passage, had a burning passion for the people and the place of God. He was devoted to God's people and wanted them to live in security in Jerusalem. Despite great opposition, Nehemiah led and completed a great project of building and repair. He secured Jerusalem and led the people in the celebratory dedication of the rebuilt walls (Neh. 12). God used this great leader to build the city of Jerusalem back up and to secure it against enemies.

We also read, in Nehemiah 12–13, about Nehemiah's role in restoring God's people under the Word of God. Through his leadership, many people fell under conviction of sin as they read from God's word, so they began to put away the evil practices they had engaged in. God's people, under Nehemiah, not only built new walls but also made a new commitment to holiness and obedience to God's word.

1. What seemed to motivate Nehemiah as he heard the news about the state of Jerusalem and wanted to go back to the land of Israel?

2. What can we learn from Nehemiah's commitment to God's people and God's place?

3. What were some of the sins that were plaguing God's people during this time? What was Nehemiah's reaction to these sins? How did he deal with them?

◇ RECAP

God did not abandon his people—even as they experienced his punishment and discipline through the years of exile. God worked through his exiled people (such as Daniel) to bring his saving blessing to the nations. Ultimately, God faithfully brought his people back to the promised land to rebuild and begin again—but it was not like the glory days of David and Solomon. His saving promises pointed to something greater than this return—something, and someone, still to come.

▼ SO WHAT?

As you conclude this chapter, jot down answers to the following application questions:

1. Summarize the roles of Ezra and Nehemiah as leaders of God's people. Compare and contrast them, and explain how God used them powerfully during these years of return to the land. How can these men serve as examples for your life, love for God, and leadership of others?

2. How was God keeping his promises to his people during this postexilic period? What promises were still clearly left to be fulfilled?

GOD'S PEOPLE—CAPTIVE AND COMING HOME
PART 2

Another major aspect of the time of the exile and the restoration that we must not overlook was the role of God's prophets in the lives of his people. The prophets' role became more pronounced during the exile and after the return. As the exile ended, these faithful men began to turn the eyes of God's people toward the future coming of a better King and a more permanent kingdom and salvation of God.

DANIEL THE PROPHET

Review pages 194–96 in *Tracing God's Story*

Daniel was a prophet who spoke to God's people during the exile in Babylon. In his vision from God in Daniel 7, he saw four beasts rising out of the sea. In verses 15–18, at least this part of the vision was explained to Daniel. These beasts represented great kingdoms that would come and reign on earth. While we do not know exactly which kingdoms were represented by this vision, we can be certain that the vision pointed to the ultimate victory of God and his people over the reign, violence, and power of all earthly kingdoms at the end of time.

It is in Daniel that the title "son of man" is given to the Messiah—Jesus—who would bring God's great rule and salvation to earth forever and ever. In Daniel 7:13–14, God the Father (the "Ancient of Days") gives all power and authority to this "son of man," who will rule over an eternal kingdom that will never be destroyed. Clearly Daniel was pointing God's people ahead to the Son of God, Jesus, who would rule God's eternal kingdom and God's people forever.

1. Who was the "son of man" whom Daniel saw? What did his role seem to be? How did God the Father interact with him?

_____

_____

_____

_____

2. How does Daniel 7 identify the four beasts that Daniel saw?

_____

_____

_____

_____

3. What seems to have been the main point of Daniel's great vision of the future?

_____

_____

_____

_____

ISAIAH AND JEREMIAH

Review pages 196–200 in *Tracing God's Story*

Isaiah ministered during the reigns of four different kings of Judah both before and after the northern kingdom (Israel) was taken into exile by Assyria (but before Judah's own exile to Babylon). Isaiah 1:1–2:5 summarizes much of what God would say to his people through Isaiah: God's judgment was about to fall on the nation of Judah because the people had largely turned away from the true and pure worship of him. But Isaiah consistently looked ahead—past the exile—to a future day of God's great salvation for his people. God did not want more animal sacrifices from his people; he wanted true hearts of repentance characterized by mourning over sin. He wanted them to turn back to him with hearts filled with true worship. This is what repentance must look like for the people of God.

Jeremiah lived in incredibly chaotic and violent times, and he himself lived through the terrible invasion of the Babylonians. He witnessed the destruction of the temple, the ravaging of Jerusalem, and the capture of God's people. Jeremiah was one more prophet, sent by God, to invite the people to repent, turn back to him, and look ahead to the promise of future salvation and a new covenant.

1. What seems to have been the source of God's anger with his people, as described in Isaiah 1? What would his punishment of his people because of their sin look like?

2. How did Isaiah 53 give God's people a picture of what his "servant" would be like?

3. What was so amazing about Jeremiah's words to God's people in chapter 31—especially verses 31–34? What did Jeremiah seem to be pointing God's people toward?

EZEKIEL THE PROPHET

Review pages 200–202 in *Tracing God's Story*

God also spoke to his people during the exile through Ezekiel. As he focused on the future salvation that God would bring to his people in a final way, he explained how the Spirit of God would have a central part in it. Ezekiel's vision of the valley of dry bones, which he recorded in chapter 37, is a picture of conversion for God's people. In order to be saved, they needed to be "spiritually resurrected" through faith in God's Son, which could happen only through the power of God's Holy Spirit. Jesus alluded to this vision in his conversation with the Pharisee Nicodemus in John 3. Jesus told this religious leader about the need to be "born again," which is the picture that Ezekiel presented in his vision. Jesus was explaining, to a man who knew God's word very well, that he needed to be converted. Without faith in Jesus and the gift of the Holy Spirit, human beings are like dead corpses lying in a valley!

1. According to Ezekiel 36:22–23, what was God's purpose and motivation as he acted on behalf of his people? Why is this incredibly important for us to remember?

----

2. What great promises of God for his people come through Ezekiel in these passages? List and explain as many as you can.

----

3. What seems to have been symbolized through Ezekiel's vision of the valley of dry bones? Can you think of any passages in the New Testament that help explain this?

MICAH THE PROPHET

Review pages 202–4 in *Tracing God's Story*

We can summarize the book of the prophet Micah by saying that it is all about *judgment* that will come soon, *salvation* that will come much later, and *repentance* that is demanded now. The conclusion of the prophecy, Micah 7:18–20, shows us an important way that Micah pointed God's people forward to a future and final salvation that God would bring to them. After several chapters filled with prophecies of God's judgment against his sinful people, Micah spoke to a final end of sin that God would accomplish for his people. He would "cast" all sins into the "depths" of the sea (v. 19). How would God do this in a final way for his people? Only through the death of his Son. Micah also pointed God's people to the person who would accomplish this great salvation for his people. He hinted at the leadership of a great Shepherd/King in chapter 5, and told us that a ruler for God's people would come from the town of Bethlehem (5:2)—a prophecy that was directly fulfilled in the birth of Jesus.

1. What did Micah say about the "ruler" (5:2) who was coming to lead God's people? What would this ruler accomplish? Where would he be born?

----

2. How did Micah characterize the true repentance and obedience of God's people, which God desires, in chapter 6? What are the true sacrifices of faithful followers of God (vv. 6–8)?

_____

_____

_____

_____

3. How do the last three verses of the book of Micah point far forward to what Jesus would accomplish on the cross? Why are these promises so big for God's people?

_____

_____

_____

_____

ZECHARIAH, JONAH, AND MALACHI

Review pages 204–12 in _Tracing God's Story_

Zechariah was a postexilic prophet who spoke God's word to God's people during a time of discouragement and disillusionment. The people had returned from the exile, but they needed God's great hope and a picture of what he would finally and ultimately do in the world. Jonah was a prophet who refused God's command to preach repentance to the Assyrian capital of Nineveh; he tried to run from God, but he was swallowed by a fish before eventually bringing God's message to the Ninevites. Malachi was probably the final prophet through whom God spoke before the coming of Jesus Christ hundreds of years later. Malachi, like the other prophets of God, was not shy about calling God's people out for their sin, but he also called them to look ahead to God's redemptive work to come.

1. In what specific ways did Zechariah point to the restoration of God's people in chapters 12–14?

_____

_____

_____

_____

_____

2. What does God's command to Jonah tell us about his heart for all nations?

_____

_____

_____

_____

_____

3. What might God's people in the time of Jesus have been waiting for, based on Malachi's words in chapters 3 and 4?

_____

_____

_____

_____

_____

RECAP

The ministry of God's prophets had a powerful effect on God's people before, during, and after the years in exile to Assyria and Babylon. These prophets—mouthpieces for God—called his people to repentance, obedience, justice, and love while also beginning to point ahead to a kingly figure (a "Messiah" or "Christ") who would fulfill all of God's great and saving promises to his people.

SO WHAT?

As you conclude this chapter, jot down answers to the following application questions:

1. Do your best to summarize the three or four main themes that you saw in all of the messages of the prophets that you studied in this chapter. How can you apply their warnings to your life as a follower of Jesus today as you see your own temptations and struggles?

2. What do the messages of the prophets say to God's people in the present? What promises about the future do they offer to God's people?

THE NEW TESTAMENT

Chapter 12

GOD'S SALVATION

Our journey through the big story of the Bible has showed us an inescapable truth: the coming of Jesus Christ to earth did not happen unexpectedly. Again and again throughout the story, God pointed his people ahead to the coming of the Messiah. In time, he fulfilled all those promises. The salvation that comes from God, centered on the person and work of Christ, is the pinnacle and climax of the entire biblical story.

WAITING ON GOD'S PROMISES

Review pages 222–24 in *Tracing God's Story*

In Luke 2:22–38, we find accounts of two faithful people who were waiting patiently for the coming of God's Messiah, the fulfillment of God's promises. One was an old man named Simeon. Luke tells us that God had revealed, by his Holy Spirit, that Simeon would see—with his own eyes—the Messiah that God had promised to his people. When Joseph and Mary brought the baby Jesus into the temple in Jerusalem, God revealed to Simeon that this was the Messiah God had promised. He realized that God's salvation had come; God had sent his own Son into the world to be the Savior of sinful people. Simeon, unlike all the generations of believers before him, got to see the person of Jesus. Anna, too, was a faithful believer in God's word, and she had been waiting for God's salvation to be fully revealed. No doubt she had pored over the words of the Old Testament prophets and knew that the Savior would be born in Bethlehem and would be a suffering servant who would die for the sins of God's people. When Anna realized that God's Savior really had come, she began spreading the good news of God's fulfilled promise to everyone who would listen to her.

1. How might it be right to understand Simeon and Anna as good examples of "Old Testament believers"—faithful Jews who believed God's promises?

----

2. How did Simeon recognize the Messiah and the completion of God's promise to his people?

----

3. What can we learn from the amazing faith of these two people, who believed God's promises and were waiting for his King to come?

THE ANGEL GABRIEL

Review pages 224–26 in *Tracing God's Story*

Before Jesus came into the world, God sent the angel Gabriel to announce the coming births of both John the Baptist and Jesus. As we see in Luke 1, Zechariah (John the Baptist's father) and Mary (Jesus's mother) both responded with songs of praise to God as they realized all that God was about to do in the world through the birth of Jesus and the preparation for his ministry through the work of John the Baptist. Mary sang out in praise to God (vv. 46–55), and Zechariah responded to the birth of John the Baptist with worship and prophecy (vv. 67–79).

Our response also should be praise when we remember the coming of Jesus Christ. The gracious Creator of the universe chose to show eternal mercy to his people. He allowed some people to repent and find forgiveness and eternal salvation through the great King and Savior that he brought into the world—his own Son. The birth of Jesus was no ordinary birth, as Gabriel's announcements remind us.

1. What did the angel Gabriel tell Zechariah about the result of John's ministry as he prepared the way for Jesus?

2. What did the angel Gabriel tell Mary about the identity and work of Jesus—the child she would bear?

3. What do you learn from the songs of praise of Mary and Zechariah that are recorded in this passage?

THE ETERNAL WORD

Review pages 226–28 in *Tracing God's Story*

John begins his Gospel (1:1–18) by declaring that Jesus, the "Word," was active in ruling and reigning as God from the beginning of time. The term that John uses for Jesus—"the Word"—is a way to talk about the eternal wisdom that is beyond this world. John tells us that, with God the Father and God the Holy Spirit, God the Son was active in the creation of the world: "all things were made through him" (v. 3). This passage tells us that the child born to Mary really was fully God. Jesus is not just a part of God. He is not merely like God. He really *is* God. The eternally existent second person of the Trinity took on human flesh and entered the world that he had been active in creating. John wants to be clear that this great God—God the Son—became truly human; he says that the Word "became flesh." John goes on to say that he "dwelt" among the people. God in human flesh (rather than a tent, like the tabernacle) came to earth to dwell with his people as one of them.

1. What does John say about Jesus's existence and power in this passage? How does he describe Jesus's role in creation?

   ----

2. How does John describe the incarnation of Jesus Christ? What specific terms does he use?

   ----

3. What is the significance, according to John, of Christ's coming to earth as a human being?

JESUS IS BORN

Review pages 228–29 in *Tracing God's Story*

In Luke 2:1–21, we discover that Jesus's birth was not the kind you might have expected for a great King and Savior. It was announced by angels, yes, but they reported it to shepherds in the field—the lowliest of workers during the time of Jesus. Also, Jesus was not born in a palace or even in a warm and comfortable house. He was born in a stable—a place where the animals were kept. By all accounts, Jesus entered this world in almost the humblest way possible. He was born not with royal fanfare but in the quiet of the night with animals in a stable.

The Son of God—Jesus—has begun his reign as King in heaven, and he will reign forever. His birth, though, reminds us that the first time he came to earth, it was as a humble servant of God's people. The Lord of all humbled himself to become human, and ultimately to serve God's sinful people in the greatest way: by dying for their sins on a cross.

1. In what ways does Jesus's birth show us the humility of his coming into this world? How was his birth not what we might have expected from the great and promised Son of David?

2. What does the announcement from the angels tell us about the significance of the coming of Jesus Christ to earth?

---

3. Do you remember one specific Old Testament prophecy that was fulfilled in the coming of Jesus Christ, and specifically through his birth?

JESUS—TRULY HUMAN

Review pages 230–31 in *Tracing God's Story*

In Matthew 3:1–4:11, we read about the ministry of John the Baptist, as well as Jesus's baptism and temptation. When we consider the fact that John was baptizing people as they repented of their sins, Jesus's baptism can be a bit confusing. Jesus was not sinful, of course; so why did he choose to be baptized by John? John wondered about this as well—and said that it would be better for Jesus to baptize him! Yet Jesus insisted. Why? It seems that, in his baptism, Jesus was intentionally identifying himself with God's sinful people, placing himself in the shoes of sinful humanity. Jesus was not sinful, but he was showing God's people that he would one day be "made . . . to be sin" (2 Cor. 5:21) for them on a cross in order to bring them lasting forgiveness and eternal life. Jesus then was tempted by Satan in the wilderness—passing the test that God's people had failed so many times.

1. How would you explain Jesus's baptism by John given the fact that John's baptism was so obviously linked to repentance from sins?

2. How would you explain what happened during Jesus's time in the wilderness as he was tempted by Satan?

----

3. What was the significance of these things happening right at the beginning of Jesus's public ministry?

JESUS CALLS DISCIPLES

Review pages 231–33 in *Tracing God's Story*

Early in his ministry, Jesus called twelve men to follow him as disciples (Matt. 4:18–22; 10:1–4). His gathering of these disciples was an intentional reflection of the way in which God had organized his work in the nation of Israel. You remember that God's people were divided into twelve tribes, based on the families of the twelve sons of Jacob (who was later called Israel). These tribes became the basis for the organization of God's people until the end of the monarchy in Israel. Now Jesus was gathering twelve disciples to follow him. Jesus was showing people that he was the "true Israel"—he would lead a new people for God, which would involve the continuous saving work of God in the world—a work now being perfectly fulfilled through him.

Jesus often spoke to the crowds, who surrounded him during many parts of his public ministry, in parables, but would then explain the parables more clearly to his disciples. Jesus's goal, it seems, was to help these twelve men understand exactly what he was all about; he went out of his way to carefully train them.

1. Why do you think the twelve disciples decided to follow Jesus so quickly? What sacrifices might they have had to make in order to truly become disciples of Jesus?

2. What do you understand as Jesus's central purpose in calling these disciples to himself at the outset of his ministry? What significance is attached to the specific number of twelve?

JESUS IN HIS HOMETOWN

Review pages 233–35 in *Tracing God's Story*

Luke 4 reminds us of an important aspect of Jesus's ministry, which he revealed clearly through the two Old Testament stories that he referenced in response to the rejection that he received from the people of Nazareth, the town where he grew up. Jesus mentioned two Gentiles—the widow who helped the prophet Elijah, and the Syrian general Naaman, who was cleansed by God from his leprosy through the help of the prophet Elisha. These two Gentiles put their faith in God—in Old Testament days—and received God's grace and favor. Jesus was telling the people that in his day—and even from the beginning—God's gifts of grace and faith are made available to all people who repent and turn to him in faith. The salvation that he had come to earth to offer was not for Jews only, but for all people! This idea of Gentile inclusion in God's plan of salvation made the people of Nazareth incredibly angry—so angry that they tried to drive Jesus out and kill him!

1. What bold claim did Jesus make about the prophecy of Isaiah that he publicly read in the synagogue in Nazareth?

------

2. How did the people of Nazareth respond to what Jesus was reading and saying about himself?

------

3. What did Jesus say that made the people of Nazareth especially angry—so angry that they tried to kill him? Why was this so offensive to them?

JESUS'S PARABLES

Review pages 235–37 in *Tracing God's Story*

Sometimes, we have the idea that Jesus told stories in order to make the truths of God clearer to people. While Jesus did speak God's truth to those who would listen, the purpose of his parables, according to Jesus, was quite the opposite. In Matthew 13:1–23, we learn that Jesus spoke in parables not to make the truth of God clearer, but so that those with hard hearts and closed minds would continue to reject the message of salvation that he brought! We know, also, that from very early on in Jesus's public ministry, the Pharisees and other religious leaders were out to kill him. The use of parables was a way for Jesus to speak the truth that he wanted to speak but in a hidden and almost coded way, so as to avoid arrest and execution before the perfect time that God the Father had ordained for his death. While Jesus spoke in parables to guard the message that he was bringing from God to God's people, there would come a day when his disciples would proclaim the truth of the gospel boldly, loudly, and clearly in all the world. In other words, parables would be over after Jesus's resurrection and ascension; the disciples would preach the gospel of Jesus Christ without any riddles or mystery.

1. What was the main point of the parable that Jesus told in this passage, according to the explanation that he gave to his disciples?

2. Why did Jesus say that he taught and spoke in parables in general? How did he use the passage from Isaiah (quoted in Matt. 13:14–15) to explain his use of parables, and what significance did this reference have?

JESUS'S MIRACLES AND HEALINGS

Review pages 237–39 in *Tracing God's Story*

Jesus's miracles and healings were all linked to his greatest purpose: helping people see his identity as the Son of God so that they could come to saving faith in him. We see this very clearly in Matthew 9. Jesus told the scribes (who were very critical of him) that he was going to heal a paralyzed man in order that they might "know" that "the Son of Man has authority on earth to forgive sins" (v. 6). Jesus performed this miraculous healing as a sign to show the people who he was. He was (and is) the "Son of Man"—the great ruler, King, and Savior of God's people, who is promised throughout the story of the Bible. He was now on earth, and he could do something far greater than make people physically well; he could forgive their sins with the authority of God, making people spiritually and eternally well!

1. What did this healing reveal about Jesus's power, authority, and identity?

2. What did Jesus seem to be even more concerned about than physical healing in the life of this paralyzed man?

3. What did Jesus seem to be trying to prove to the people watching this healing?

4. What might this passage tell us about Jesus's purpose in performing miracles on earth?

JESUS AND THE RELIGIOUS LEADERS

Review pages 239–41 in *Tracing God's Story*

In Matthew 15:1–20, we see that representatives of the scribes and the Pharisees, two sets of strict Jewish religious leaders in Jesus's day, approached Jesus to condemn him and his disciples for not keeping the "tradition of the elders" with regard to hand washing (v. 2). It is important to note that what they were describing was *not* an official part of God's law; it was an added tradition—something that their forefathers had called God's people to do as an extra part of Jewish ritual. Jesus responded to the criticism of the religious leaders by telling them that they had made a habit of making God's word "void" by relying on their traditions more than keeping the heart of what God's word taught (v. 6). He gave another example of the way in which the religious leaders had twisted the commandment about honoring one's father and mother, and had made an exception to it. This exception seemed spiritual, as it released people from honoring their parents if they were devoting themselves to God. But Jesus said that this actually denied God's law and therefore was wrong. Jesus ended this confrontation with some very strong words to the Pharisees and scribes. He linked them with the hypocrites that Isaiah prophesied about—people who praised God with their lips but had hearts that were far from giving genuine worship to him.

1. What was the specific issue that these religious leaders seemed to have with Jesus and his disciples that led them to confront Jesus? Was this issue related to God's law? How do you know?

----

2. How did Jesus respond to these religious leaders? What problem did he identify with their hearts?

3. How did Jesus go on to teach his disciples based on this encounter with the religious leaders?

JESUS AND THE LAW OF GOD

Review pages 241–43 in *Tracing God's Story*

At the end of Jesus's Sermon on the Mount (Matt. 5–7), Matthew tells us that all of the people who heard it were amazed—not only at the teaching itself, but at the "authority" of Jesus, the one who taught (7:28–29). He taught in a different way than the scribes and the Pharisees; he taught as if he were the one who had written the law (in a way, he had). Jesus was interpreting the law of God authoritatively through himself.

To respond to the teaching of the Sermon on the Mount, people first need to respond to Jesus. The first response is not to say, "How must I do this?" but, "Whom must I trust and put faith in so that I can do this?" The answer is Jesus—God's Son.

Jesus also was clearly saying that he is "fulfilling," not "abolishing," the Law and the Prophets of the Old Testament (see Matt. 5:17). Jesus came not to bring a completely new order for God's people but to fulfill all of God's commands and promises in himself. Jesus was affirming the beauty and truth of the law of God, and showing how, through faith in him, God's people can fulfill and obey God's law in *greater* ways than the people of the Old Testament.

1. How would you describe Jesus's interaction with God's law in this sermon? What was he careful to explain about his purpose in coming and teaching? What was he *not* trying to do with God's law?

   _____

   _____

   _____

   _____

2. What, in general, was Jesus calling God's people to do? How was he calling them to live, according to the end of Matthew 5?

   _____

   _____

   _____

   _____

3. Describe the response of the people to Jesus after he ended his sermon. What was it about him that amazed them?

   _____

   _____

   _____

   _____

JESUS ENTERS JERUSALEM

Review pages 244–45 in *Tracing God's Story*

In Zechariah 9:9, the prophet speaks about the King coming to his people while riding on a donkey's colt. This prophecy was very specifically fulfilled when Jesus entered Jerusalem (see Matt. 21:1–9). This was probably the absolute height of Jesus's public popularity, and there was no doubt that many people would have made him their king at this time. Jesus, though, was not there to reign—at least not in the way that many people thought. He had come to Jerusalem to "reign" from a cross, where he would die, and then to rise again to break the power of sin and death forever. Just days after the people shouted out to Jesus as the Son of David, they would cry out for Pontius Pilate to crucify him.

As Luke 22 begins, we see the tragic fall of one of Jesus's twelve disciples, Judas Iscariot. Judas became possessed by Satan, and he set out to betray Jesus to the religious leaders of the Jews. In exchange, they gave him money, and the plot to kill Jesus began. While Judas was obviously guilty and sinful, even his betrayal was part of God's great plan. Jesus had to go to the cross and be killed if God's people were really going to be saved and forgiven.

1. How were specific prophecies about Jesus Christ fulfilled in his entry into Jerusalem? What does this tell us about who Jesus ultimately is for God's people?

2. What is the purpose of the Lord's Supper, which Jesus gave to his disciples—and to all of his people—in Luke 22?

3. How was Jesus clearly approaching the moment that he saw as his chief purpose in coming to earth?

JESUS'S CRUCIFIXION

Review pages 246–47 in *Tracing God's Story*

John 19 gives us a full account of Jesus's trial, crucifixion, death, and burial. Here we see that he endured terrible physical suffering at the hands of human beings. He was whipped, beaten, mocked, and tormented with a crown of thorns. Then he was literally nailed to a cross—hung on a wooden structure with pointed metal nails that were driven through his hands and feet. The physical suffering that Jesus endured was torturous, and he endured it purely out of love for God's people and out of hope for what he was going to accomplish for them. But we need to understand that the physical suffering of Jesus did not nearly equal the spiritual suffering that he endured in his sacrifice. When Jesus hung on the cross, God the Father turned his back on his Son in wrath, and the guilt of God's people was counted as Jesus's own. As a result, he endured all of the bitterness and utter agony of guilt, shame, and the unrestrained wrath of God against every sin of God's people for all time. This is why, in another Gospel account, Jesus is recorded to have cried out the words of Psalm 22:1: "My God, my God, why have you forsaken me?" (see Matt. 27:46). This was eternal suffering, the full experience of the horrors of hell.

1. How is the Gospel of John very clear about the reality of the terrible physical suffering of Jesus?

----

2. How is the Gospel of John very clear about the reality of Jesus's physical death?

_____

_____

_____

_____

_____

3. What does the death of Jesus mean for God's people?

_____

_____

_____

_____

_____

JESUS'S RESURRECTION

Review pages 248–50 in *Tracing God's Story*

John 20 is an account of the resurrection of Jesus, as well as several different appearances that he made to his followers after he rose again. Neither John nor any of the other Gospels record the actual event of the resurrection. All of them are unified, though, in their simple and clear affirmation that Jesus really did rise bodily from the dead. Jesus really did die on the cross; everyone around him during his death saw this without a doubt. Likewise, Jesus really did rise from the dead; he appeared to hundreds of people who became witnesses of this amazing miracle to all the world. Jesus also rose with an obviously physical body. In John 20, we see that Jesus allowed Thomas to literally touch the wounds he had received on the cross. Another passage records him eating fish with his disciples (Luke 24:42–43). Jesus's body was physical, but it was also a special resurrection body. His disciples were kept from recognizing him at various points, and he was able to appear suddenly, and even enter a room that had locked doors. The witness of John 20—and the other Gospel accounts—is that Jesus really rose bodily from the dead.

1. How does John show the wonder of Jesus's followers as they were confronted with him in bodily and resurrected form? Why were some of them slow to believe? Can you identify with their doubts?

2. How does John's Gospel account make it obvious that Jesus really rose again in bodily form?

3. Keeping in mind what you have learned about the story of the Bible, what does the resurrection of Jesus Christ mean for God's people?

AFTER JESUS'S RESURRECTION

Review pages 250–52 in *Tracing God's Story*

Luke 24:13–49 relates how the risen Jesus taught his disciples how the story of the Bible pointed to him. First to two men on the road to Emmaus and then to all his disciples, he unfolded the entire story, with himself as the main character and the climax! Jesus told the men on the road that it was "necessary" for the Messiah to suffer, die, and be raised from the dead, for the Old Testament demanded it (vv. 26–27). Verse 27 also provides a summary of the message that Jesus gave to these men: he explained to them from all the Old Testament the things "concerning himself." It seems that he went through the entire Bible (Old Testament) and showed them how all of the story was moving toward *him*. He did the same thing for his disciples, showing them that everything that was written in the Old Testament needed to be fulfilled in his work (vv. 44–47). Jesus retold the whole story of the Bible to his disciples and showed them how he was its main character.

1. What were the two men whom Jesus met on the road struggling to understand and believe? Why is it not difficult for us to identify with these men?

_____

_____

_____

_____

2. What did Jesus rebuke these men for? What had they failed to understand and believe?

_____

_____

_____

_____

3. What was the general point that Jesus made to these two men and to all of his disciples in this chapter of the Gospel of Luke? What does this tell us about the way that we should read and study our Bibles?

_____

_____

_____

JESUS'S FINAL DAYS ON EARTH

Review pages 252–53 in *Tracing God's Story*

As Jesus prepared to return to heaven with God the Father, he gave his disciples a very important charge—they would be the ones who would begin to carry the message of his salvation to every part of the world. The specific call of Jesus was for them to "make disciples" of all nations (Matt. 28:19). These disciples, who had given everything to follow Jesus, were now instructed to multiply themselves by sharing the gospel and "teaching" (v. 20) others everything that Jesus has taught them. They were to do this in "all nations" (v. 19)—this was a global call to make disciples and followers of Jesus Christ. Finally, this disciple-making process was to be accompanied by the covenant sign of baptism, which was to be done in the name of the Father, Son, and Holy Spirit (v. 19). Jesus, fully God and fully man, was calling his disciples to make more followers of him as they boldly proclaimed his message in all the world. Because of the depth and significance of the gospel message—that God truly saves sinners through his Son—this message needed to be shared in every corner of the earth.

1. In what ways is Matthew's postresurrection account different than Luke's and John's accounts? Why might this be?

---

2. What does Matthew tell us about the disciples themselves as Jesus prepared to commission them?

---

3. What was the specific call and commissioning of Jesus about? What did he command his disciples to do?

⬡ RECAP

We have come to the climax of the story of God's redeeming work in the world for his people: the coming, life, death, and resurrection of Jesus Christ. He is the Son of God, who took on flesh to serve as the perfect representative for God's sinful people. Jesus obeyed God's word perfectly in the place of God's people, and he died on the cross in their place to bear the punishment for their disobedience. Then he rose from the dead, giving assurance that all who repent and put their faith in him will live forever under his perfect reign.

⬇ SO WHAT?

As you conclude this chapter, jot down answers to the following application questions:

1. Discuss three specific prophecies—or promises—from the Old Testament that were explicitly fulfilled for God's people through the coming of Jesus Christ. How can the Old Testament expectations about the coming Messiah expand your view of Jesus, as well as your joy in the gospel?

2. Explain how Jesus is the ultimate answer to the expectations that these prophecies or promises formed in the hearts and minds of God's people as they waited for the Messiah in faith.

GOD'S CHURCH
PART 1

As Jesus prepared to return to heaven forty days after his resurrection, his disciples seemed to not quite understand what his work in the world would look like in the coming years. They even asked him if he was going to "restore the kingdom to Israel" (Acts 1:6), probably wondering whether it was time for God to bring the glory and power back to his people on earth. But Jesus had a very different plan for his people and the message of the gospel until he comes again.

THE CHURCH BEGINS

Review pages 256–58 in *Tracing God's Story*

In Acts 1:1–11, Jesus corrected the misguided view of his disciples and told them what their key role would be after he returned to God the Father in heaven: *witness*. They would be witnesses to him—his life, death, and resurrection, which is the full message of the salvation of God that has come to earth. Jesus told the disciples that their witness would go out from Jerusalem to Judea to Samaria and then to all the ends of the earth. In other words, God's promise to Abraham was about to be fulfilled in the greatest way yet—God's great message of salvation would finally begin to bless the peoples of the earth as the disciples spread the message of Jesus Christ everywhere. Specifically, God would work through his *church*. He did not plan to gather a great army for himself or raise up a great political leader like David or Solomon. God would entrust his glorious gospel to his people, who collectively would make up the church—which would be built and grown through the proclamation of the message that Jesus entrusted to his disciples.

1. What does the disciples' question in Acts 1:6 tell you about their mindset? What might they still have been a bit confused about?

2. What did Jesus tell them that their role would be, according to Acts 1:7–8?

3. How does this passage set up the rest of the book of Acts? What should we expect to happen in the rest of this book?

THE DAY OF PENTECOST

Review pages 258–60 in *Tracing God's Story*

Jesus had told his disciples to wait in Jerusalem to be "baptized" by the Holy Spirit. They had already put their faith in him; this baptism was to be a special gift of God for them; it would be a special empowering for them as they began the important work of bearing witness to the death and resurrection of Jesus Christ as the centerpiece of the saving work of God in the world. In Acts 2, we read what happened when the day of this baptism finally came. At the celebration of Pentecost in Jerusalem, many people were gathered from all over the world. God's Holy Spirit descended on the disciples, and something amazing happened: they started proclaiming the gospel of God's salvation through Jesus in different languages—languages that they had previously not known! Thanks to this "gift of tongues," everyone gathered in this place began to hear the message of Jesus Christ. The Holy Spirit had come with power, and something big was about to happen. As Peter preached the gospel, three thousand people came to faith—and the New Testament church was born.

1. What miracle happened at Pentecost? What were the disciples able to do as the Holy Spirit acted powerfully through them?

2. How would you summarize the content of Peter's sermon? What was he trying to show and prove to the people in Jerusalem?

3. What do you learn about the early church in Acts 2:42–47?

PETER'S PREACHING

Review pages 260–62 in *Tracing God's Story*

In Acts 3:1–4:22, we find an account of the powerful witness, in both preaching and healing, of Peter and John in the early days of their proclamation of the gospel of Jesus Christ. Peter showed the people the implications of the coming of Jesus Christ. He is clearly the only way to salvation, and all who reject him are rejecting the God of all of history. This is the God who sent his Son to fulfill his work of salvation in the world; all people must accept this Savior! The witness of Peter's preaching should remind us of an important application today: the Bible really is one story—God's story—of his saving work in the world and in the lives of his people. Peter saw the promises of God to Abraham and to his people through the prophets coming together gloriously in the person and work of God's Son, Jesus Christ. On this basis, Peter proclaimed Jesus to the people of his day. He told them that God had continued and fulfilled his work in the world through his Son. This amazing gift was the basis of Peter's call for repentance and belief.

1. What seems to have been Peter's and John's main focus, even though God sometimes used them to bring healing to people in miraculous ways?

2. What seems to be the main point in Peter's sermon in Acts 3:11–26? How did he connect the message of Jesus Christ to the entire story of the Bible?

3. What seems to be the main point and thrust of Peter's speech to the elders and scribes of the Jews in Acts 4:8–12?

STEPHEN'S WITNESS

Review pages 262–64 in *Tracing God's Story*

In Acts 6:8–7:60, we are introduced to another important disciple of Christ, Stephen, and observe his defense before the Jewish religious leaders after his arrest. As Stephen preached, he used the temple of God as a direct path to Jesus. He reminded the people that the God of the universe does not live in man-made temples (7:48); he is a God who cannot be contained. He then told the Jewish leaders that they were responsible for killing the prophets in the past and, most recently, for killing the Messiah from God: Jesus Christ himself! As you can imagine, the Jewish leaders reacted extremely strongly and viciously to this biblical indictment. In a crazed fit of anger and rage, they dragged Stephen outside the city and stoned him to death. This was a terrible murder, committed by people who could not accept the fact that they had missed the point of the Old Testament Scriptures, which was to point them to Jesus Christ—the very man that some of them had helped crucify.

1. How is the ministry of Stephen described in Acts 6? How did God use this man in powerful ways for the growth of his gospel?

---

2. Stephen's speech was long! Try to summarize the main progression of his sermon before the Jewish council. Who did he mention? Why did he choose to mention them? Where did he end?

3. What was the response of the Jewish leaders to Stephen's sermon? What does this tell you about their hearts?

SAUL'S CONVERSION

Review pages 264–66 in *Tracing God's Story*

Saul, a young and very bright Pharisee, was opposed to Jesus and his followers in every way. He probably saw the gospel as a way for people to get out from under obedience to the law; he saw no room for the free grace of the cross or the teaching of the resurrection of Jesus from the dead. So Saul led the way in trying to snuff out the witness of the gospel in the world through terrible persecution. Acts 9, however, records one of the most unlikely conversion stories in all of history. While on the road to Damascus, Saul was struck to the ground by a blinding light and heard the voice of Jesus speaking directly to him. He was confronted by the risen Lord Jesus Christ, who declared to Saul that he had been persecuting *him*. Saul was temporarily struck blind and obeyed Jesus's command to go into Damascus and wait to be told what to do. Jesus then appeared in a vision to a disciple named Ananias, who—by God's power—prayed for Saul's sight to return. Saul received spiritual sight as well as physical sight as he put his faith in Jesus and began to serve him under the new name of Paul.

1. Read the opening verses of Acts 8. What about Saul made him a most unlikely convert to Jesus Christ?

    ....

    ....

    ....

    ....

2. What does the story of the conversion of Saul tell us about God?

    ....

    ....

    ....

    ....

3. What was God's special purpose for Saul, as he explained to Ananias (Acts 9:15–16)?

    ....

    ....

    ....

    ....

PETER AND CORNELIUS

Review pages 266–67 in *Tracing God's Story*

Peter had been faithfully bearing witness to Jesus Christ among the Jewish people in Jerusalem, but as we see in Acts 10, God had an important lesson for Peter to learn. In a vision, Peter saw various "unclean" animals and heard a voice telling him to "kill and eat" (vv. 12–14). As Peter was trying to understand this vision, some men arrived from Cornelius—a Roman centurion—asking Peter to go with them to see their master. When Peter arrived at the house of Cornelius, he finally realized the meaning of the vision that God had given him on the roof. Cornelius was a Gentile; he was not part of the covenant family of Abraham by blood. Nevertheless, he wanted to be saved through faith in Jesus Christ. God was teaching Peter a foundational lesson about the gospel: faith in Jesus is available to all people through the gift of God's Holy Spirit. It is not only for the Jews; Jesus truly came to save all those who repent of sins and trust him as Lord and Savior. In the presence of Peter, Cornelius and the people of his house received the Holy Spirit and came to full faith in Jesus Christ (v. 44). Peter went away with a powerful and important message to share with the Jewish believers in Jesus: even Gentiles can now be accepted into God's family if they repent and believe in Jesus.

1. What was Peter's initial reaction to the command to "kill and eat" in his vision on the roof? What did this vision seem to symbolize?

2. What lesson was God teaching Peter through this vision? How did God then ask him to apply this truth in real life?

3. What was the significance of what happened in the house of Cornelius when Peter went to visit him? How was this a beautiful fulfillment of God's promise to Abraham hundreds of years before?

PAUL IN ATHENS

Review pages 268–70 in *Tracing God's Story*

Not long after God taught Peter about the availability of salvation to all people—including Gentiles—we see the apostle Paul sharing the gospel and preaching the message of Jesus Christ in a very Gentile context. In a sermon in the Areopagus of the Greek city of Athens, recorded for us in Acts 17, Paul made his way to Jesus, but he got there in a different way than Peter did in Acts 2. Paul was speaking to Gentiles—people who were not familiar with the story of the Old Testament. Still, they too could turn to Jesus in faith even though they did not have the history of the Jewish people and information about the prophets of the Old Testament. It should be slightly encouraging to us that even the great apostle Paul was met with mixed result in Athens. Acts 17 tells us that some people believed the message of Jesus that he was proclaiming; God did his work of conversion in the hearts of a few. But many laughed at him when he spoke of the resurrection of Christ. Finally, some were willing to hear him talk more about this subject but were not yet at the point of personally believing in Jesus.

1. How does Luke (the author of Acts) describe the context of Athens? What kind of place did the Areopagus seem to be?

2. What kind of audience was Paul addressing as he shared the gospel of Jesus Christ in this passage?

3. How do you see Paul's approach differing from Peter's in Acts 2?

THE CHURCH IN ACTS

Review pages 270–71 in *Tracing God's Story*

As Paul was moving closer to some of the trials and legal troubles that would finally bring him to imprisonment for the gospel in Rome, he set out on a trip to Jerusalem (Acts 20:17–38). En route, he stopped to meet with the elders of the church in Ephesus. From the simple fact that Paul could call together a group of elders from this church, we can gather that an immediate effect of the spread of the gospel and the conversion of many people across Asia Minor had been the formation of local churches in every city and/or town where there were believers in Jesus. A result of the ministry of the apostles was that local gatherings—probably meeting in homes—sprang up in places like Ephesus, Corinth, Thessalonica, and Philippi. People in these towns began to gather regularly for corporate worship—the teaching of God's word, the singing of praise, the celebration of the Lord's Supper, and times of prayer to God. By the time of Acts 20, we see—just as the apostles had directed—that these churches were ruled by elders who could govern well. As we consider this reality of local churches springing up in the towns that had been reached by the apostles, we begin to see God's surprising plan for the growth and health of his gospel in the world.

1. What happened, regarding local churches, in the days following the resurrection and ascension of Jesus?

2. What does this tell you about God's chosen way of making his gospel go forth in the world?

---

3. What was the content of Paul's speech to the Ephesian elders, and how might this give us a hint of what we will see in the Epistles of the New Testament?

THE END OF PAUL'S LIFE AND MINISTRY

Review pages 272–73 in *Tracing God's Story*

In Acts 27–28, Luke recounts Paul's journey to Rome as a prisoner and his house arrest there. While imprisoned in Rome, Paul was guarded and watched, but he had a certain amount of freedom; for example, he stayed by himself—something that was not allowed for all prisoners (28:16). He lived at his own expense, talked with many people, and continued to share the gospel of Jesus Christ "with all boldness and without hindrance" (v. 31). This final verse of Acts shows us Paul's faithful witness—even to the very end of his life. He was not a perfect man, of course, but he was faithful; he never strayed from the gospel call that Jesus Christ had committed to him. Our final glimpses of Paul show him teaching about Jesus to the local Jewish leaders in Rome and welcoming people to his house (or prison cell) as he continued to bear bold witness to the salvation that comes only through the Lord Jesus Christ.

1. What have been some of your main observations about the ministry of Paul? How does Acts 27–28 show us Paul remaining true to his calling from God?

----

2. What seems to have been Paul's situation in the city of Rome? How did he continue to share the gospel and tell people about Jesus in this great city?

◆ RECAP

After Jesus's ascension to heaven, we see the powerful work of the Holy Spirit in gathering believers together, empowering the apostles to preach the gospel, and allowing the message of Jesus to go forward and spread with power—from Jerusalem to Judea to Samaria and to the ends of the earth. Believers in Jesus began to gather in their local communities to worship, hear God's word, and proclaim the gospel. The New Testament church had begun.

▼ SO WHAT?

As you conclude this chapter, jot down answers to the following application questions:

1. How does the book of Acts seem to explain and describe how the words of Jesus to his disciples (in Acts 1:8) were fulfilled in the years after his ascension? Explain the way that those words clearly came true through the witness of the apostles as the gospel spread. What should be your reaction to these words of Jesus as one of his followers today?

Chapter 14

GOD'S CHURCH
PART 2

The Lord Jesus's apostles not only ministered by traveling about in order to preach the gospel and establish churches. They also wrote letters to those churches and to particular believers in order to instruct God's people more fully in the gospel and give guidance to the church leaders as they shepherded the people in those early days. These letters, the New Testament Epistles, were inspired by the Holy Spirit, so they are authoritative and powerful for our lives today. In this chapter, we will look at the message of some of these epistles.

GALATIANS

Review pages 276–78 in *Tracing God's Story*

Galatians is a short but powerful book. It does not take long to see the problem in the Galatian church that Paul wrote to address! It seems that some people—probably legalistic Jews—had come into the church and were preaching a "different gospel" (1:6) than Paul had proclaimed to these people. They were telling the Galatians that while their faith in Jesus was good, they needed to follow Jewish laws and customs to really be in good favor and relationship with God. It seems that this kind of teaching was having a powerful effect on the Galatian believers—many of whom were probably Gentiles. Paul, on his part, was obviously filled with righteous anger at this kind of teaching. He uses strong language to denounce these false teachers (see 1:8–9), but also goes after the Galatian believers for falling prey to this kind of false teaching (3:1–5). His entire letter is focused

145

on correcting the false teaching that had permeated this church and on bringing the Galatian Christians back to the true gospel of Jesus Christ, which is received by faith alone.

1. What seems to have been happening in the church at Galatia, according to what Paul says in 1:6–9?

2. How does Paul defend his own gospel ministry in 1:11–24, and what purpose might this defense serve as he writes this letter?

3. What does Paul present as the true message of the gospel in Galatians 3? Why is this so important for God's people to remember?

PHILIPPIANS

Review pages 278–80 in *Tracing God's Story*

Paul wrote to the church at Philippi to encourage the Christians there and to challenge them to keep growing in their faith in Jesus Christ. While this was a healthy church, it had problems with disunity. There seems to have been, at least in some pockets of the church, a lack of full gospel unity between believers. Paul goes as far, in chapter 4, as to call out two women by name in order to encourage them to "agree" in the Lord (v. 2)! This is why Paul spends time, in 2:1–11, calling for unity in Christ and then reminding the people about the great example of Jesus Christ's humility. He ultimately put his interests behind the interests of God's people as he laid down his life in sacrifice for them. God's people should not engage in petty fights and arguments with one another but should seek to count others "better" than themselves (2:3), agreeing in the Lord and seeking unity in the gospel of Jesus Christ. The Philippians seemed to have some room for growth in this area.

1. What does Paul say about the church at Philippi as he opens his letter? What encourages him about their faith?

2. Why might Paul have needed to encourage the people in this church about the purpose of his imprisonment?

3. What does the beginning of chapter 2 tell you about one problem in this church?

ROMANS

Review pages 280–82 in *Tracing God's Story*

The book of Romans has been called the greatest theological treatise that Paul ever wrote. One of his purposes in writing this letter was to clearly explain the gospel. But he had a more practical reason too. Paul, according to chapter 1, wanted to visit the Christians in Rome. It seems that he may have wanted to use Rome as a kind of launching point for a gospel ministry journey to Spain. So Paul wrote to encourage the Romans with the truth of the gospel, as well as to tell them to get ready for his coming and to prepare to support him as he moved on from there into other nations of the world with the gospel message.

Some common themes and phrases show up in Paul's introduction to the letter (1:1–5) and his conclusion (16:25–27). One is the idea of the gospel of Jesus Christ bringing about the "obedience of faith" for "all the nations" (1:5; 16:26). Paul wrote to explain the gospel of Jesus Christ, but also to make the argument that, because of its truth, it must be taken to all nations. Paul wanted the Romans to understand the importance of people everywhere hearing about Jesus and obeying the gospel by putting their faith in him and following him completely.

1. How would you summarize Paul's opening greeting in his letter? What does it tell you that this letter will be about? How does Romans 16:25–27—the other bookend of this epistle—tell you about Paul's main point for this letter?

2. What is the big problem of all humanity that Paul seeks to identify in Romans 1:18–3:20?

3. What is God's great solution to this problem, and how does Paul explain the fact that God's justice is maintained as he justifies and saves sinners?

_____

_____

_____

_____

1 CORINTHIANS

Review pages 282–85 in *Tracing God's Story*

We saw that the church at Philippi was fairly healthy; in contrast, the church at Corinth was full of problems. Ancient Corinth was, by all accounts, a wild city—full of sin, partying, and all kinds of perversion and corruption. In fact, there is evidence that the term *Corinthian* came to be used as almost a synonym for a person who was sexually immoral and sinful! Given this context, it is perhaps not surprising that God's people in the church at Corinth seem to have struggled to stay separate from the world in which they lived.

Paul begins his letter by commending the Corinthians for their amazing spiritual gifts, which had come graciously from God. Paul even goes so far as to say that the Corinthians are "not lacking" in any spiritual gift (1:7). But sadly, while the church at Corinth was richly gifted, it was far from being a mature church. In fact, Paul saw it as incredibly *immature*. In chapter 13, he makes references to many of the rebukes that he has given to the Corinthians and shows them how they are not fulfilling the greatest gift and greatest sign of maturity: *loving* one another!

1. What does Paul commend the Corinthians for as he begins his first letter to them?

_____

_____

_____

_____

2. What are some of the issues that Paul boldly addresses in chapters 1–3?

---

3. What are some of the other issues that were going on in this church, as revealed in chapters 5–6?

PAUL AND TIMOTHY

Review pages 285–87 in *Tracing God's Story*

Paul wrote the book of 2 Timothy not to a church but to a person. Timothy was most likely serving as what we would now call the "pastor" of the ancient church at Ephesus. He was young, and he seems to have been prone, at least in some ways, to timidity and shyness. Timothy had been by Paul's side; Paul mentions him as a faithful friend and colaborer in the gospel with him. He had learned from the aging apostle and gathered everything he could from his example as a faithful preacher of God's word. Now Paul had come to the end of his life. The words that we have in 2 Timothy are probably some of the final words that Paul ever wrote. His goal in this epistle was to pass on to Timothy the most important things for his future years of gospel ministry.

Paul's focus, not surprisingly, is on the gospel of Jesus Christ. In 1:14, we see Paul calling Timothy to "guard the good deposit"—the gospel word that had been given to him. As Timothy carried on the work of God in the world—even long after Paul was gone—he needed to teach and defend the true gospel.

1. What is the legacy that Paul reminds Timothy about as he begins this letter?

----

2. What seems to be most important to Paul about Timothy's ministry throughout this letter?

----

3. What does Paul warn Timothy about and tell him to watch for in ministry?

JOHN'S EPISTLES

Review pages 287–89 in *Tracing God's Story*

Paul was not the only apostle whom God inspired to write letters to his people. Another was the apostle John, who wrote the Gospel of John, three letters that are part of our New Testament, and the book of Revelation. In the first of his three letters, John is firm in calling believers in Jesus to understand that to continue to "walk" in the darkness of sin while claiming the name of Jesus Christ simply does not work (1:6). A changed heart leads to a changed life. He encourages believers to test themselves to see if they truly have genuine faith. John offers the doctrine test, especially as the believers to whom he writes deal with heresies, false teaching, and even deceitful spirits. He tells them that anyone who "denies that Jesus is the Christ" is not from God (2:22). Later, John discusses the importance of confessing that Jesus Christ has truly come in the flesh; this is part of the essential doctrine of the Christian church. There is also the love test. John says that people who have believed in God and who claim to follow Jesus must bear fruit by really loving one another deeply. Christian love is, for John, a huge "proof" of genuine Christian faith, along with right doctrine.

1. What echoes of the Gospel of John do you see in 1 John 1–2? How can you tell that these books were written by the same author?

2. How would you summarize some of the major points that John seems to be making in these chapters?

3. Why are these points very important for the church to hear in every age of history?

PETER'S EPISTLES

Review pages 289–91 in *Tracing God's Story*

God also used the apostle Peter to bring his good word to his people as the church was growing across the ancient world. In the first of his two letters, Peter wrote to "elect exiles" (1 Pet. 1:1). It seems that these followers of Jesus Christ—all over Asia Minor—were facing various levels of persecution (this is a big theme in 1 Peter). Mainly, this persecution seems to have been verbal abuse, social alienation, and insults, though some of those to whom Peter wrote may have been facing literal beatings or imprisonment for their faith. Peter's words, then, were directed to "spiritual" exiles—people who did not really belong to the world in which they lived. One of Peter's central messages to people living in this kind of situation is the call to holiness. Peter is not shy about calling believers to honor the Lord Jesus by holy and obedient conduct as they wait for their heavenly home with God.

1. What does Peter's greeting tell you about the way that he viewed the people to whom he wrote? What might have been some of their struggles and hardships?

----

2. What are some repeated themes that you see in these first two chapters of 1 Peter?

THE BOOK OF HEBREWS

Review pages 291–94 in *Tracing God's Story*

The book of Hebrews, perhaps more than any other book in the New Testament (with the possible exception of Romans), gives us an expansive look at how not only prophecies but also events and practices of the Old Testament are ultimately fulfilled in the person and work of Jesus Christ. In fact, some biblical scholars have even described the book of Hebrews as several extended sermons on passages of the Old Testament, sermons designed to show how these passages are perfectly and wonderfully fulfilled in Jesus. Hebrews helps us see many connections between God's work in the past and God's work in the present (through his Son) that we might otherwise miss. On this note, we probably can summarize the theme of the book of Hebrews as simply "Jesus is *better*!" That is the declaration of the book's anonymous author as he considers many practices, customs, laws, and pictures of the Old Testament. He sees Jesus, God's Son, and all that he did for the salvation of God's people as the infinitely better completion of all the "shadows" of the Old Testament that pointed forward to him.

1. Why does the author of Hebrews say that Jesus is even better than Moses as a leader for God's people?

2. In Hebrews 3–5, how does the author of Hebrews present Jesus as the great high priest for God's people? What does he mean when he uses this term for Jesus? How does he argue for this point?

THE BOOK OF JUDE

Review pages 294–96 in *Tracing God's Story*

The little letter of Jude—written by a brother of Jesus—is often overlooked. But it should not be! Jude offered an important call to the Christians of his day—and to followers of Jesus today. Jude tells us his purpose for writing the letter in verse 3: he says that he wanted to write about the common salvation that he shares with his audience, but he felt compelled to write instead about the need to "contend" for the gospel. Jude quickly goes on to explain the reason for this call. Certain people, he says, had crept into the community of God and were enticing others to abandon their faith and pursue sin instead of holiness (v. 4). Considering this, the true gospel of Jesus Christ, and the life of obedience that accompanies it, must be defended and protected (v. 3). Much of the body of Jude's letter, after this purpose statement, is made up of examples from history of people who turned away from faith in God toward sin, false belief, and the deception of God's people. Jude mentions Cain, Korah, and the cities of Sodom and Gomorrah (among others). His point is to remind God's people that there is a danger—in every age—of turning away from true faith in God into sin and wrong belief. Jude is calling his readers to be on their guard and to hold on to the true gospel of Jesus.

1. What does Jude say that he intended to write about? What, though, is the purpose that he says he felt compelled to actually write to his audience about?

2. Do you notice any repeated themes, phrases, or words that Jude seems especially focused on in this letter? How would you summarize some of the main, and most important, points that he makes?

◇ **RECAP**

God speaks to his people by divinely inspired letters ("epistles") written by the apostles to the early churches. These letters explain and apply the gospel to the lives of God's people, calling them to believe, obey, love one another, bear witness to Jesus, and resist false teaching and heresy. These letters still guide us today as members of churches that follow in this apostolic tradition.

▼ **SO WHAT?**

As you conclude this chapter, jot down answers to the following application questions:

1. Describe some of the ways that particular epistles that you studied in this chapter (mention at least two or three) connect the work of Jesus Christ to God's promises to his people throughout the Old Testament. Does this connection strengthen your confidence in the promises of God today?

   ----

2. How do the epistles help us understand the Bible as one big story of God's saving work in the world? Why is it important to see ourselves as part of the Bible's story—as members of the New Testament church?

Chapter 15

GOD'S ETERNITY
PART 1

All of God's big story has now been told except for one part: the return of
Jesus Christ and the final judgment of the world. God is simply waiting for
the perfect time to send his Son back to earth to signal the end of history.
God's word has much to tell us about this still-future part of the story. In
this chapter, we'll look at the way in which some Old Testament passages
pointed forward to the end of all things, along with a few passages in the
Gospels and New Testament Epistles. In the next chapter, we'll survey what
the book of Revelation teaches about the end.

ISAIAH'S PROPHECY

Review pages 299–301 in *Tracing God's Story*

In Isaiah 60, the prophet Isaiah tells us repeatedly that the nations of the world will
come in a united way to the worship of the one true God. He describes nations coming
to the light of God (v. 3) and the "wealth" of the nations flowing into God's place (v. 5).
Isaiah speaks of the kings of the nations ministering to God's place in a significant way
(vv. 10–11). And he looks forward to a day when the descendants of the enemies of God's
people will bow down before God and worship him along with God's people (v. 14). Isaiah
is telling God's people that, for all eternity, there will be a multiethnic gathering of people
that will sing God's praises. God's final plan involves bringing all kinds of people to faith
in his Son. The eternal experience in heaven will be a great congregation of people from
every nation in the world—people who truly acknowledge and worship Jesus Christ the
Lord! They will share in the beauty of God's perfected and glorious kingdom forever.

1. What is the role of the nations and the peoples of the earth in this passage? Why would it have been so significant—and surprising—for Isaiah to focus so much on these groups of people in his prophecy?

2. What will God's role be in this perfected place for his people? How will he rule over them in perfection and glory?

ZECHARIAH

Review pages 301–3 in *Tracing God's Story*

Like Isaiah, the prophet Zechariah pointed God's people forward to the conclusion of God's story, but with a slightly different emphasis. He spoke to the postexilic community of God's people in Israel, seeking to encourage them by looking far ahead to a future day of God's final salvation, judgment, and restoration of his people. In Zechariah 14, the prophet offers great hope to God's people: the promise of God's perfect and final judgment against the nations that have attacked and oppressed them. He describes God going out as a warrior to fight and defeat the nations who have opposed both him and his people. The promise of God through Zechariah, in other words, is that one day, all wrong will truly be set right. Evil people and evil nations will be judged, and God truly will bring his perfect justice to all the earth. Zechariah also puts before God's people the promise of God's perfect and final peace and security, which will come to his people in a lasting way. Verse 11 shows us that, one day, the great city of God will never again be destroyed, and that Jerusalem (the place for God's people) will dwell in perfect security. This is a promise of lasting peace and safety for God's people. They will dwell securely with their God forever and ever—and the nations of the world will come to him in worship and humility.

1. What specific words of hope does Zechariah offer to God's people in this passage?

....

....

....

....

2. What do you see about the promises of this prophecy that reminds you that Zechariah looks ahead to a future day—one that we have not yet fully experienced?

....

....

....

....

3. How should this passage give hope to Christians today as they still await the final coming of Jesus Christ and God's perfect victory and salvation for his people?

....

....

....

....

DANIEL

Review pages 303–5 in *Tracing God's Story*

The prophet Daniel pointed ahead to the day of God's future judgment of all the earth. In Daniel 7, we read that the prophet received a vision of four beasts that come out of the sea. These beasts, we are told, are great national powers that wage war on the earth out of the desires for domination and conquest. In the book of Revelation, these beasts are all rolled into one final great beast at the end—one whom we often refer to as the "antichrist." This part of Daniel's vision is showing God's people that, during the last days before Christ's return, we should expect times of great violence, conflict, and sinfully motivated conquest and chaos. World powers will never stop competing and battling until the very end of time.

Ultimately, though, all earthly powers will finally be silenced. Daniel's next vision is of God himself—the "Ancient of Days"—taking his seat on his throne to judge every human being who has ever lived. Here is a picture of the final judgment of the world. "Books" will be opened, which probably refers to the exposure of all the deeds that have been done on earth throughout all the ages. God himself—in all his terrifying holiness and glory—will judge all humanity in a final way and establish his judgment and salvation in all the earth forever.

1. What specifically do Daniel's visions seem to be about? What are the central things that he sees?

2. What are these visions meant to teach God's people? Why do you think God chose to communicate these things to us through the prophet Daniel?

3. What difference should it make to our lives that we know that this is what the end will look like? In other words, how does a vision of the final chapter of history make a practical difference in our lives today?

THE OLD TESTAMENT AND THE RESURRECTION

Review pages 305–7 in *Tracing God's Story*

The Old Testament also points ahead to another important aspect of the conclusion of God's story, an aspect that is explained much more clearly in the New Testament: *resurrection*. There is little material in the Old Testament that explicitly lays out how the final resurrection will work, but there are hints about it there. For example, Psalm 16 points us strongly to the reality of the resurrection of the Messiah—God's "holy one" (v. 10), as David calls him. Peter, preaching on this psalm in Jerusalem many years later, pointed the Jewish people to the grave of David, reminding them that he could not have been talking about himself when he said that God's Holy One would not see "corruption" (Acts 2:29–31). David, speaking prophetically, was pointing in this psalm to the eternal resurrected life of God's Messiah—Jesus. Jesus would truly die, but he would rise again from the dead. In Job, we see the future hope of the resurrection of God's people more specifically. Amid his lament and cries to God, Job stops and remembers his ultimate future hope. He looks far ahead into the future, to a day when his "Redeemer" will stand on the earth (19:25). He believes that, long after his "skin has been . . . destroyed," he will nevertheless somehow see God in his "flesh" (v. 26). Job's hope is in the fact that one day God's people also will be raised from the dead. Job pictures a day when the great divine King will stand on the earth, and God's people will rise from the dead to see him with their eyes and to serve him forever.

1. Where is the resurrection mentioned in Psalm 16? How did Peter interpret this reference, and to whom did he apply it? What does this tell us about King David, and about the way that he wrote and spoke?

2. What seems to be Job's hope, as evidenced in Job 26? How does he explicitly seem to be hoping for a physical and future resurrection?

THE NEW TESTAMENT AND FINAL JUDGMENT

Review pages 307–9 in *Tracing God's Story*

The Gospels tell us that Jesus spoke about heaven, judgment, and eternal life on many occasions, but it was in his Olivet Discourse, recorded for us in Matthew 24–25, that he talked about the final days in the most detail and with the heaviest concentration. Jesus's words about "tribulation" (suffering) in 24:9–14 connect and agree with what Daniel prophesied in Daniel 7. They also agree with what John prophesies in the book of Revelation. Before the end comes, it seems there will be times of suffering, persecution, and hardship on earth. We do not know how extensive this tribulation will be or exactly how long it will last. We should assume, though, that things will get worse in the world before Jesus returns, but that his gospel will continue to go forward with power!

Twice in the Olivet Discourse, Jesus speaks of his glorious and globally significant return to earth. In Matthew 24:30–31, he talks of coming in the clouds, accompanied by the trumpet call of the angels. Then, in 25:31, Jesus again speaks of coming "in his glory" and sitting on his glorious throne. The picture of his return that Jesus presents to us is one of complete glory, power, and rule over all the earth. He came once as a humble baby to die on a cross for sinners; he will return as the conquering and ruling King and Judge over all creation.

1. What are some of the events and signs that Jesus identified for his disciples as he described what life will be like as the end of the story of the world approaches?

2. How did Jesus urge his disciples to hope and to be ready for these coming times? What is the only way to prepare for the tribulation, the return of Jesus Christ, and the final judgment of the world?

----

3. How can we apply these chapters to our lives today as followers of Jesus Christ?

----

2 THESSALONIANS AND THE LAST DAYS

Review pages 309–11 in *Tracing God's Story*

Another portion of the New Testament that offers insights about the conclusion of God's story is the little letter of 2 Thessalonians. Paul wrote this epistle to an early church that was struggling with how to think about the end times. Some of the believers in this church thought that they might have missed the return of Jesus Christ. Paul wrote to correct their thinking and to help them understand a terrible figure who will come in opposition to the gospel. In the letter, Paul teaches us that God and his people will be attacked, opposed, and battled in essentially every way until the final return of Jesus Christ. Paul describes what is coming as a "rebellion" (2:3), which will be led by the "man of lawlessness," whom he goes on to describe. This passage connects with what Jesus said in Matthew 24–25 and with what John writes in Revelation. The witness of all of Scripture agrees on this point. Until the very end—and probably with increasing intensity—the true gospel of Jesus Christ will be opposed by the evil forces of this world and by Satan himself. Therefore, Paul calls God's people to "stand firm" (2 Thess. 2:15). The man of lawlessness will come; Paul wants the believers in Thessalonica to be aware of this fact. But they can also know that the gospel is true. Their faith is sure, and they need to hold firmly to all that they have been taught about Jesus Christ.

1. How does Paul describe the man of lawlessness? What will he do in the world, and what seems to be his ultimate purpose and goal?

_____

_____

_____

_____

2. Why does Paul teach the believers in Thessalonica about this person?

_____

_____

_____

_____

3. How does Paul comfort and encourage the believers as he closes chapter 2 of this letter?

_____

_____

_____

_____

1 CORINTHIANS AND THE RESURRECTION

Review pages 311–14 in _Tracing God's Story_

Earlier, we noted that the Old Testament Scriptures offer hints about bodily resurrection. As we look at Paul's writing in 1 Corinthians 15, we see this future resurrection hope made much more explicit. For Paul, the hope of resurrection for believers in Jesus is completely grounded on the fact the Jesus himself really rose bodily from the dead. He is the "firstfruits" of believers who have died—the one who rises first and sets the example and the model for everyone who will follow him into resurrection life (v. 20). To put this in slightly different words, we have no hope that we will be raised from the dead someday if Jesus Christ was not truly raised first! Paul even goes one step further. He says that if Jesus has not been raised from the dead, we are still in our sins (v. 17). If Jesus stayed dead, that means that his sacrifice for sin was not enough to be accepted by God. But that is not the case. Jesus *did* rise from the dead, proving that the sacrifice for sin that he made on the cross was accepted by the holy God. His resurrection was God's vindication of his Son; it proved that by Jesus's sacrifice, sin really is completely paid for and death has been defeated for all who put their faith in him.

1. What is the significance of the resurrection of Jesus Christ, according to Paul? What would it mean for believers in Jesus if he had not been raised from the dead?

2. How does Paul explain the kind of resurrection body that believers in Jesus will receive? What comparisons and metaphors does he use to explain his teaching?

DAVID AND THE "FOREVER KINGDOM"

Review pages 314–16 in *Tracing God's Story*

Let's go back to the Old Testament one final time as we prepare for our final chapter (which focuses on the book of Revelation). In 2 Samuel 7, God made a promise to David that ultimately pointed to the "forever kingdom" that is still to come. He promised David that his house and his kingdom would stand forever before him—a promise that his kingly line would never go away. It is not surprising that many of the people of Israel came to expect that another human king would rise to lead God's people and return the nation of Israel to the glories of the days of David and Solomon. What they did not realize was that the kingdom of God—the forever kingdom that he had promised to David—would be much greater and far more glorious than the earthly city of Jerusalem! Jesus, then, was not the "Son of David" that many of God's people expected. He was, humanly speaking, descended from David, but he came saying very clearly that his kingdom was "not of this world" (John 18:36). Jesus came humbly—to serve God's people and to save them from their sins by dying on a cross for them. Here was a king who would not reign from a palace in Jerusalem, but would reign from a bloody cross, where he would fight the greatest battle on behalf of God's people—a battle against Satan, sin, and death. This King would rise again and return to heaven, there to begin reigning from the right hand of God the Father and waiting to finally establish the eternal kingdom of God after his return to judge the earth.

1. Describe and summarize some specifics of the promise that God made to David in 2 Samuel 7. What did he promise to do?

2. Were there any conditions attached to this great promise to David?

3. What effect might this promise have had on God's people leading up to the time of Jesus? How would they have probably expected God to fulfill this great promise to David?

◈ RECAP

The Old Testament Scriptures, as well as the New Testament Gospels and Epistles, point to the glorious eternal future for God's people who have placed their faith in God's Son. What lies ahead for God's faithful people is resurrection life in the new heaven and new earth, where they will reign with Christ and rejoice forever in the presence of their Savior. That part of the story is yet to begin; we await the return of Jesus as King and Judge.

◈ SO WHAT?

As you conclude this chapter, jot down answers to the following application questions:

1. Take one of the themes that we have learned about in this chapter relating to "God's Eternity" (resurrection, judgment, worship, place, forever kingdom, etc.) and explain how, through Jesus, it can fill believers with great hope.

---

2. Discuss why this rightly placed hope is so important for Christians today. In other words, why should you think more often about the glorious hope that lies ahead for you through faith in Jesus Christ?

GOD'S ETERNITY
PART 2

To get the best possible picture of what lies ahead, we need to turn to a study of the book that gives the largest and most complex explanation of the conclusion of God's saving work in the world: Revelation. In this chapter, we will seek to get a solid and thorough overview of what this book teaches about the last things and about what God's people can expect at the conclusion of his big story.

THE BOOK OF REVELATION

Review pages 318–20 in *Tracing God's Story*

The book of Revelation is a direct "revelation" from the Lord Jesus Christ to the apostle John, who was exiled on an island because of his faith in Jesus. In other words, John did not come up with this on his own. This vision was a gift from God to John, and, through John, to his church. Jesus gave John this vision to show God's people the "things that must soon take place" (1:1). We should assume, then, that much of what John writes about in this book concerns events that have not yet taken place. There is a future-oriented focus in Revelation. God is showing his people, through John's vision, his plans for what is to come. John's vision gives the church a glimpse into the final chapter of God's story.

1. In Revelation 1:1–3, what does John tell us about the visions that he is about to describe for us? What are they meant to show God's people, according to John's words?

----

2. What should be the response of readers of this book, according to John? What is promised for those who read this book and pay careful attention to it?

GOD'S THRONE ROOM

Review pages 320–22 in *Tracing God's Story*

Revelation 4–5 shows us that Jesus Christ is the one who will bring about all of God's eternal purposes for both judgment and salvation in the days to come. Everything, then, that will come after this in Revelation, as confusing as it may seem, is part of God bringing his purposes to pass through the person and work of Jesus Christ, his Son. Most fundamentally, Jesus will accomplish the eternal salvation of God's people through what he has already done. He is praised and worshiped, as chapter 5 closes, for his work on the cross. He was slain—and he ransomed a people for God by his blood (v. 9). This "Lion" (v. 5) and Judge is also the "Lamb" (v. 6) who died for God's people. Jesus will be both these things as he brings God's story to its conclusion. Revelation 4–5, then, shows us all that is coming—in the rest of the book and in the days ahead in the story of God's work in the world. Jesus is preparing to bring about—and complete—all of God's sovereign purposes for perfect judgment and for final salvation of those who belong to Jesus by faith.

1. What is happening in Revelation 4? What is the reason for the great praise and worship that we see happening in this chapter?

2. What happens in Revelation 5? What seems to be the meaning of the drama that occurs here?

---

3. What is the reason for the songs of praise and worship in chapter 5, and how are these songs different from the song in chapter 4, which focused mainly on God as Creator?

THE SEVEN SEALS

Review pages 322–24 in *Tracing God's Story*

In Revelation 6:1–8:1, the Lamb begins to open the seven seals on the scroll that John first saw in chapter 5. These seals are the first set of three remaining "sevens" in the book of Revelation. All these series of sevens are meant to describe the perfect and full judgment of God on the earth. The seven seals come first, then the seven trumpets, and then finally the seven bowls of God's wrath that are poured out on the earth. Each series of seven ultimately represents the same thing—God's judgment—but subsequent series seem to build on the previous ones, with each progressively becoming more intense and global (the final bowls, for example, seem to describe judgments that will each make a complete end of the entire earth). The first four seals are judgments symbolized by horses, which probably signify God's judgments that come through the forces of war, death, disease, and famine. The fifth seal shows the need for judgment as God's faithful martyrs wait to see his perfect judgment revealed. The sixth seal brings about the vanishing of the sky itself as the rulers of the earth grow aware of the coming wrath and judgment of the Lamb. Revelation 7, though, gives us a picture of

God's redeemed people kept safe and delivered from God's final judgment through faith in Jesus Christ.

1. What seems to be happening as the seven seals are being opened in this passage? What do these seals generally represent?

2. Where is the seventh seal finally opened? What does this placement mean for the purpose of chapter 7?

3. How might the question at the end of chapter 6 help us understand the purpose of chapter 7?

THE SEVEN TRUMPETS

Review pages 324–26 in *Tracing God's Story*

Because of the similarities between the plagues on Egypt and the trumpet judgments in Revelation 8–9, we should take these to be against people who choose to trust the things of earth for their security rather than God. In these judgments, God affects everything that people might be tempted to rely on for security. While the first four trumpets bring forth judgments that seem to affect the earth generally, the fifth and sixth trumpets bring judgments that particularly affect those who have chosen to follow Satan instead of Jesus Christ. Both have to do with the influence of demonic beings—Satan's evil and violent servants in the world. They torment and abuse their followers, and then lead demonic armies in wars that take thousands and thousands of human lives. God is sovereignly allowing Satan to torment and torture those who have chosen to sinfully follow him rather than Jesus.

1. How do the judgments described in this passage remind you of the judgments God poured out on Egypt through ten plagues in the book of Exodus?

2. How do the first four trumpet judgments differ from the fifth and sixth ones?

3. What is surprising about the final two verses of this passage (Rev. 9:20–21)? What are these verses meant to teach us?

SATAN RAGING

Review pages 326–28 in *Tracing God's Story*

Revelation 12 gives us insight into Satan's work in the world throughout history—and into the future. The first part of this passage (vv. 1–6) shows Satan's opposition to and attacks against God's people. Stepping back in time, John tells us that after Satan was thrown down from heaven (v. 9), he came down to earth in great "wrath, because he knows that his time is short!" (v. 12). Satan's response to his defeat (and his knowledge of his inevitable judgment by God) was to devote himself to creating as much violence, sin, and destruction on earth as he could. God has allowed him a certain amount of time before his final judgment, and so Satan is spending that time making war on all those who belong to Jesus for as long as he can. Even during this powerful activity of Satan, though, God's people continue to be "nourished" and protected by God (vv. 13–14). Those who belong to Jesus Christ should acknowledge and understand the activity of Satan, but they do not need to be terrified or tormented by him. His time is short, and he knows it. As we will see later in the book of Revelation, there will come a day when he will finally be thrown down forever by Jesus, never more to torment or attack the people of God.

1. As best as you can understand, what is symbolized by the woman in this passage? What is the dragon's (Satan's) attack on this woman all about?

2. What do we learn about Satan from the battle that takes place in heaven?

3. What is Satan's response to knowing that his time on earth is short?

THE ANTICHRIST

Review pages 328–30 in *Tracing God's Story*

Revelation 13 introduces us to another evil force or person that Christians are to expect as the return of Jesus and the final judgment of the world draw nearer—the "antichrist." The first beast in Revelation 13 is a composite of the four beasts that the prophet Daniel saw—a terrible combination of all their powers. This means it is probably best to see this beast as a great world leader or ruler, one who will be greater than all the mightiest world powers of all time. This will be a political ruler—an antichrist who will exalt himself over all the world and seek to bring all peoples to serve and worship him.

A second beast comes up in the second part of this chapter. This beast is distinct from the political ruler, the antichrist. His role seems to be specifically religious, as he seeks to direct all the world in the organized worship of the antichrist. People everywhere are marked with the symbol of allegiance to this beast, and they cannot buy or sell anything unless they are under that mark. The goal of both beasts, who are in service to Satan, is obviously total domination of the lives, hearts, and souls of humanity as they oppose God and demand human worship and allegiance.

1. What does the first beast seem to accomplish in the world? What is the response of the world to his rule and activity?

----

2. What does the second beast seem to accomplish in the world? What does he seek to get the people of the world to do?

3. Who are the only ones who are safe from the influence of these beasts? Why are they safe?

THE CONQUERING LAMB

Review pages 330–32 in *Tracing God's Story*

In Revelation 19, we observe two meals. The first of these meals should be very encouraging to believers in Jesus Christ. As he has done before, John puts before us the multitude of people who have confessed Jesus as Savior and now gather in praise to him. These people have been invited to the great "marriage supper of the Lamb" (v. 9). This image—a marriage supper—has appeared in several places in the Bible story; it is always a beautiful and climactic feast. We should note that those who attend this marriage supper are dressed in "fine linen," which, John explains, is the "righteous deeds of the saints" (v. 8). These good deeds are, of course, gifts from Jesus Christ; no one can earn saving favor with God by his or her own strength.

The second meal of Revelation 19 is a bit grotesque. An angel calls out to the birds overhead to gather for the "great supper of God" (Rev. 19:17), which comes as he judges sinners who have rejected Jesus as Lord and Savior. The description of these people covers everyone—from kings down to ordinary people—who has refused the rule of Jesus. The two beasts are defeated and devoured as well. All in all, there is no real battle—the enemies of God are simply destroyed, and the birds that gather overhead devour their flesh (v. 21).

1. What is encouraging to Christians about the feast that is described in Revelation 19:6–10? In the vision, what is the response to God of those invited to the feast? How are they dressed for this meal?

2. What do you notice about the description of Jesus in verses 11–16? How is this different from the way we normally picture Jesus?

3. What do verses 17–21 teach us about sin and judgment?

THE MILLENNIUM

Review pages 332–35 in *Tracing God's Story*

Revelation 20:1–3 shows us the event that signals the beginning of the millennium (the thousand-year reign of Christ). It is the binding of Satan so that he is unable to deceive the nations any longer. Satan is pictured as being bound with a chain and then thrown into a pit, which is closed and sealed over him. Verses 4–6 then describe Christ's millennial reign. Satan is bound during this time, and it seems that Christ rules on earth with the resurrected saints of God, who have been raised to share in Christ's reign. This is a time of peace on earth as Christ visibly and powerfully manifests his reign as the rightful King of all the world. Finally, in verses 7–10, Satan is released to make one last attempt in battle against God the Father and his Son, Jesus Christ. Even after the visible reign of Christ on earth for a thousand years, many people still flock to follow Satan in his battle. It does not go well for Satan and his army, though; they are consumed with fire from heaven and then thrown into the lake of fire to be judged eternally.

1. What event seems to signal the beginning of the millennial reign of Christ? What is the goal of this binding?

2. Who is pictured as reigning along with Christ during the millennium?

3. How is the final battle extremely anticlimactic?

A GOOD ENDING

Review pages 335–37 in *Tracing God's Story*

Revelation 21–22 shows us the new world that will follow the judgment. In the first 8 verses of chapter 21, John focuses on the newness of everything that he sees. The old heaven and earth are gone; they have finally "passed away" (v. 1). God has made an end of this fallen world and has initiated his new creation—a new heaven and new earth for his people. His people, too, are new; they are "adorned" like a bride for him (v. 2), no longer stained with sin but made ready to live in eternal and perfect relationship with him. In fact, "all things" are new (v. 5). God's salvation for his people is finally complete in this future scene, just as judgment is final for those who have rejected him.

1. In Revelation 21:1–8, what shows us that God's judgment of sin and his salvation of his people are finally complete?

2. What echoes of Old Testament promises and prophecies do you see in the description of the new Jerusalem from verse 9 onward?

3. How might the numbers and the descriptions of the heavenly city be functioning in this passage? What might John be trying to tell us by including these details?

⬡ RECAP

John's vision in the book of Revelation gives us the Bible's most extensive teaching on the last days, the end of the world, and the triumphant return of Jesus Christ as Savior, King, and Judge. We know that there is a good ending to this story, as God's redeemed people will witness the end of sin and death—and Jesus's final defeat of Satan. This world will end, and Jesus will make all things new. Believers in Christ await that day with joy, faith, endurance, and hope.

▼ SO WHAT?

As you conclude this chapter, jot down answers to the following application questions:

1. Explain the theme of Jesus as Lion/Lamb (King and Savior) that continues throughout the book of Revelation. Give a few specific examples of passages that display this theme clearly in the book.

---

2. Why must we remember Jesus as both the Lion (the King) and the Lamb (the Savior)? What dangers might you avoid in your walk with the Lord by remembering that Jesus is both Lion and Lamb—full of both power and grace?

Also Available from the Theology Basics Series

The Theology Basics series is a collection of books, workbooks, and videos designed to provide an accessible introduction to the study of biblical truth—systematic theology, biblical theology, and biblical interpretation.

For more information, visit **crossway.org**.